AUSTRALIA'S Cape York PENINSULA

Clifford & Dawn Frith

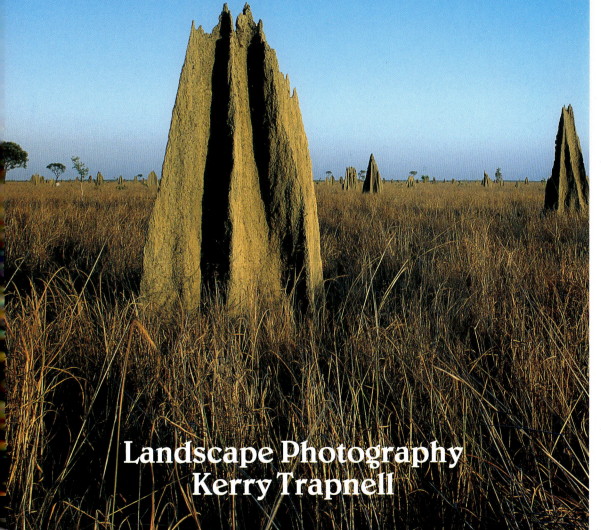

Landscape Photography
Kerry Trapnell

Published in Australia
by FRITH & FRITH Books
'Prionodura', P.O. Box 581,
Malanda, Queensland 4885
Telephone (070) 96 8105

National Library of Australia
Card Number ISBN 0 9589942 6 9

Copyright © C. B. & D. W. Frith, 1991.

Apart from any fair dealing for the purpose of private study, criticism, or review, as permitted under the Copyright Act, no part of the book may be reproduced by any process without the written permission of the publishers.

First printed 1991

Other books in this series:

Australian Tropical Rainforest Life
Australian Tropical Birds
Australian Tropical Reptiles and Frogs
Australian Tropical Reef Life
Australian Tropical Butterflies

To the memory of
Arthur Thorsborne 1912–1991
in appreciation

Torresian Imperial Pige

Foreword

The Cape Today

The tide of European development that swept most of Australia faltered on the shore of a few great islands of wilderness. One of those that to this day remains unconquered and unsubmerged is the remote and beautiful land of Cape York Peninsula – Australia's north-eastern frontier.

It has survived because it was, and still remains, a difficult environment, hostile to European concepts of land use. Its soils are almost universally poor; its pasture lands though often rank with grass, are the least productive in tropical Australia; though blessed with high rainfall it is cursed with long seasonal drought. For a century it has been the realm of a handful of pastoralists barely eking out a living from what has been basically the harvest of wild or semi-wild cattle, and, until the massive bauxite mining operations began at Weipa about thirty years ago, a few miners involved in small scale operations for gold. There have been a number of attempts to change this, the most notorious of which were the ill-advised and large-scale pasture developments of the late nineteen-sixties and early nineteen-seventies which left a legacy of degraded land from Bamaga to Lakeland Downs. None were successful. They were the product of a mentality that assumed that only the lack of motivation, knowledge, and resources of an incumbent population, had hampered the development of the region. Time has proven, however, that the traditional practices of the pastoralists were more suitable and sustainable than the methods of those who attempted to impose development systems from more southern areas which relied on massive alterations of the native ecosystems.

Undeterred by past failures, the development ethic still flourishes in the belief that there must be some way to turn the empty vastness of the Peninsula into riches or civilised order. In quick succession in the last two decades have emerged proposals for oil palm and cashew plantations, wood-chip operations, timber harvesting, silica quarrying, defence air bases, tourist resorts, and most recently, a space base. Perhaps only the land speculators have really profited to date, and it is the need to benefit from speculative investments that now, more than ever, drives the increasingly frenzied search for development options.

Tragically, the Aboriginal people, for so long careful custodians of the landscape, and now driven to confinement in its most barren pockets, have often been forced, in attempts to advance themselves economically and socially, to developments modelled on European concepts of appropriate land use. The attempts have mostly failed, leaving both the land and its Aboriginal communities the poorer. To overcome the problems of an impoverished land base, and to address the injustices of the past, Aborigines today are more determined to take control of their own destiny and the ownership of land has become their dominant political demand.

In the pastoral industry too, still the dominant land use of the Peninsula, great changes are afoot. The campaign to eradicate brucellosis and tuberculosis has resulted in large-scale de-stocking, and the herds of the future will largely be confined behind fences, eliminating much of the long-term pressure by semi-feral stock on sensitive stream frontages and other environments. Although large scale clearing operations have recently returned to the southern Peninsula, it is being increasingly realised that there is little benefit in such land use. Future pastoral development will see more emphasis on extensive development in which tree cover is retained while seeds of legumes and grass are sown underneath them.

Ironically, it is certain that it is the wilderness and wildlife values of Cape York Peninsula, so long under attack as impediments to progress, that will ultimately prove to be the source of those long-sought riches for the region. The increasing scarcity of these resources in the rest of the world is guarantee of that. We have a history of most-valuing that which we have lost or are about to lose. Cape York Peninsula will long remain one of the least crowded and most natural places on a planet in which quality of life threatens, for the majority of the world's individuals, to become that of the battery hen. The world will eventually beat a path to its door, and therein lies the challenge.

It is natural that the nation's National Parks of the future must come mostly from the large remaining virgin areas such as the Peninsula. These will be the basis, together with sympathetic management of surrounding lands, of the region's future prosperity. Management of these reserves will require increasing skill, perception, and determination. They will be under threat from an increasing range of species introduced in attempts to increase cattle production, the dramatic effects of the rapid change in fire regimes since European settlement, and increasing visitation. Sadly it appears that even the land-rights aspirations of the Aboriginal people will, under current proposals, be largely focused on that other victim of European oppression, the remaining wild lands as expressed in the existing National Parks.

It is fervently to be hoped that we will have the wisdom to find solutions and practices that will favour both social justice for the people of Cape York Peninsula, of all races, and retention of most of its beauty and richness of wildlife and scenery. This small book, in fostering understanding and concern for those values, will be a contribution to progress in that direction.

Peter Stanton
Biologist
Cairns

Introduction

Cape York Peninsula is one of the remotest, wildest, least populated and unspoilt tropical wilderness areas of Australia. It is an area of unsurpassable beauty, of unique geological formations, an immense diversity of habitats, and a flora and fauna of great biological significance. It is a land of changing moods and colours; the clear blue winter skies dramatically differing from the foreboding monsoonal summer rain clouds (lower left of front cover); the silvery sand dunes contrasting with the yellow or red soils of plains and plateaux, and the vast marine plains and salt flats with the green lushness of vine forests.

Location and History

Located on the north-eastern tip of Queensland, north of latitude 16°, this triangular-shaped Peninsula covers an area of about 130,000 square kilometres. The biogeographic region is defined by the southern limits of Stringybark forests, *Eucalyptus tetrodonta*. It extends from Cooktown on the east coast south-westwards to Lakeland and the upper reaches of the Palmer River, and then westwards along the Palmer and Mitchell Rivers to the coast (see map, page 71). On the west of the Peninsula is the Gulf of Carpentaria and on the east the Great Barrier Reef and Coral Sea.

Cape York itself (page 4, above), located at $10^\circ41'$S $142^\circ32'$E, is the northernmost extremity of continental Australia. It is only about 150 kilometres south of the Papua New Guinea mainland and is separated from it by the, island rich, Torres Strait. The word Torres originated from the early Spanish navigator, Luis Vaez de Torres, who first found a way through the Strait from the east in 1606. The Torres Strait Islands, some twenty four kilometres north-west of Cape York, are separated from the mainland by the Endeavour Strait, named after the vessel the HMS *Endeavour* of Captain James Cook fame. Cook first sailed through the Strait in 1770 and landed on Possession Island, just off the Cape York coast (page 4, below). Here, on 22nd August 1770, Cook hoisted the English flag and claimed the east coast of Australia for George III and England. A monument marks the site of this historical ceremony. Today, Possession Island is a National Park of great historical significance and, apart from some damage caused by gold miners between 1897 and 1906, it remains much the same as it was in Cook's day. During this voyage the ship's botanist, Joseph Banks, made the first significant biological exploration of the Peninsula, mostly when the vessel was under repair in the Endeavour River at Cooktown, after it had been holed on Endeavour Reef on the 11th June 1770. Captain Cook named such areas as Cape York, Newcastle Bay, Temple Bay, Cape Grenville and Cape Weymouth.

Twenty years later another great navigator, Captain William Bligh, and his few faithful crew members, reached Cape Weymouth. This small band of men, victims of the infamous HMS *Bounty* mutiny, sailed across the Pacific Ocean in a small open boat towards the Australian mainland. On 29th May 1790 they landed on the small island off Cape Weymouth and named it Restoration (page 5, above). In 1802 Captain Matthew Flinders charted the waters around the coast in great detail. Other explorations of great historical significance included the voyages of the HMS *Beagle* under Commander John Lort Stokes in 1841 and the HMS *Fly* with naturalist J. Beete Jukes aboard in 1843.

The first land explorations were made by Ludwig Leichhardt who travelled down the Mitchell River in 1845 and, three years later, by the ill-fated Kennedy Expedition. This was one of the most famous but gruelling epics of all early Australian explorations. Edmund Kennedy and his party of twelve set off on the 5th June 1848 from Rockingham Bay, south of Cairns, to travel some 1000 kilometres north to the tip of Cape York. On 12th November they reached Weymouth Bay, where eight weak party members remained. Kennedy, a young Aborigine called Jackey Jackey, and three others proceeded northwards. On 24th November Kennedy and Jackey Jackey left the others near Shelburne Bay and went on. Kennedy was speared several times by Aborigines of the Jadhaigana people near the Escape River and died on 11th December in the arms of Jackey Jackey who continued alone and eventually reached the supply boat at Albany Island (page 5, below). Only two of the men at Weymouth Bay survived; others are interred on Albany Island.

In 1864-5 Frank and Alexander Jardine, and eight other men, attempted to herd some 250 cattle from Rockhampton, in southern Queensland, to the new administrative settlement of Somerset on the tip of Cape York. Near their destination they discovered a wide fast-flowing river, later named after them, and with great difficulty crossed it. They reached Somerset on 13th March 1865, despite hardships and heavy loss of livestock. Frank Jardine continued to run cattle around Somerset and was its Governor Resident for some time. He is buried on a beach below Somerset with his Samoan princess wife, Sana Solia. Two ancient cannons on the headland beside Albany Pass (page 5, below) today mark this settlement. Other events of historical significance include the discovery of gold on the Palmer River by William Haan in 1872; R. Logan Jack's geological survey from Cooktown via Coen, the Archer and Escape rivers to Somerset in 1979-80; and the construction of the Cape York Overland Telegraph Line in 1886-87. Following narrow trails and guided by this telegraph line an Austin was the first car to reach the Cape, on 31st October 1928!

The Aboriginal people of Cape York Peninsula, of which there were several hundred kin groups, have lived there for more than 30,000 years. Their history, or Dreamtime, is chronicled over a vast area of sandstone rock art about Laura, some of which may be the oldest on earth., The earliest artform is thought to be at least 13,200 years old. These outstanding galleries of paintings extend through a vast network of caves and were named the Quinkan Galleries by Percy Tresize, a pilot who discovered them in 1959.

In 1605-1606 the Dutch Ship *Duyfken* (Little Dove) under Captain Janszoon sailed down the west coast to Cape Keerweer. This arrival represented not only the first record of Europeans on the Peninsula but, with the death of nine crew members from Aboriginal spears, also the first hostilities between the two races. Such conflicts continued for the next three centuries, particularly during early explorations. Coastal Aborigines tended to be sedentary seafaring fisherman and hunters of dugongs and turtles; inland folk were nomadic, travelling in search of plant and animal foods. It was their custom to burn land, perhaps to facilitate travel and improve visibility, particularly in areas of dense grassland, and also to flush out wallabies, goannas and other animal foods. Today this practice is still carried out by Aborigines and, more drastically, by pastoralists (lower right of front cover, **opposite**, & see page 19).

ear Blue Lagoon, Lakefield

Tip of Cape York, from north

Looking toward Endeavour Strait & Possession Island, from Red Island Point

Cape Weymouth & Restoration Island

Albany Pass & Albany Island, from Fly Point

Climate and Geology

Cape York Peninsula has a monsoonal climate with a mean annual rainfall that exceeds 1000 millimetres in most areas, with peak falls (average about 1800 millimetres) on Cape York, Iron and McIlwraith Ranges and areas just north of Cooktown. It is wettest during the hotter north-west monsoons of December to April. The rest of the year experiences drought, except along the east coast where the south-easterly winds bring showery weather even during the colder winter months of May to August. September and October are notably dry. Average daily summer maximum temperatures are about 30-32°C and the average winter ones between 15-20°C.

Some 160 million years ago, Australia formed part of a vast southern continent known as Gondwana which also included New Zealand, South America, South Africa, India and Antarctica. This huge land mass started to fragment, and continents drifted slowly apart. Australia broke away from Antarctica some fifty million years ago. New Guinea is a more recent island and was uplifted when the Australian and Asian plates converged. During the last twelve million years the sea level of the Torres Strait has fallen several times to expose land bridges permitting an interchange of flora and fauna between the two islands. Thus, many plants and animals on the Peninsula, and elsewhere in tropical north Australia, also occur in New Guinea; although most are still characteristically Australian derived from Gondwanan ancestors.
The Great Dividing Range, consisting of igneous and metamorphic rocks, runs down the spine of Cape York Peninsula, from the north near the Olive River southward on the eastern side of the Peninsula, reaching a maximum height of about 800 metres in the McIlwraith Range near Coen. North of the Olive River the range continues under the sea along the coast towards the tip of Cape York. Much of the Peninsula is low-lying, consisting of two major sedimentary basins – the Carpentaria and the Laura. About two thirds of the Peninsula on the western side of the range comprise of the low plateaux and undulating plains of the Carpentaria Basin that rarely exceed 150 metres in elevation with a complex intricate network of rivers flowing westward into the Gulf. The Laura Basin, on the south-eastern side of Peninsula, has extensive areas of salt flats, grasslands, wetlands, and rivers that flow into Princess Charlotte Bay (see page 10).

There are some dramatic landscapes on the Peninsula. Some examples are the outstanding limestone karst country north of the Mitchell River (**right above**), the strongly-dissected sandstone escarpments and plateaux around Laura (see page 2); the enormous granite boulders at Cape Melville (**right** & upper right of front cover), the dazzling white silica sand dune cliffs at Elim Beach, north of Cape Bedford (**opposite above**) and also at Cape Grenville and Orford Ness, and the vivid red bauxite cliffs at Ussher Point (**opposite below**) and on the west coast near Weipa. The deposits of bauxite ore in the Weipa area are vast, covering an area of about 3000 square kilometres. At Cape Flattery more than a million tonnes of sand are mined annually, mostly for the Japanese and Korean glass industries. Gold has been mined sporadically, from a number of fields on the Peninsula, since its 1872 discovery in the Palmer River.

HABITATS
Beaches and Dunefields

The coast of Cape York Peninsula is spectacular and diverse from the impressive red bauxite cliffs at Weipa and Ussher Point (**page 7, below**), to wide deltaic estuaries of major river systems, dense mangrove forests near the mouth of the Escape River, immense sandy cliffs north of Cape Bedford (**page 7, above**)) and in Shelburne Bay, to prominant rocky headlands near Cape Melville (upper right of front cover). Long stretches of silvery sandy coral beaches curving to form sweeping bays, are a feature of the east coast such as Captain Billy Landing (**opposite above**).

Beaches and exposed coastal sand dunes, commonly referred to as the strand, are continuously subjected to battering by the sea and wind and are subject to severe erosion. Many species of creepers and shrubs colonise this coastal sand and help stabilise it. Hairy Spinifex Grass and the handsome purple flowering Goat's-foot Convolvulus, *Ipomoea pes-caprae* (**opposite above**), are early colonisers. By spreading their runners (spinifex) or stems (convolvulus) outward in all directions the plants assist in holding newly-deposited sand together. The Goat's-foot leaf is shaped liked a cloven hoof – hence its name. Convolvulus leaves constitute a useful Aboriginal bush medicine – heated leaves are applied to the skin as a treatment to reduce infection on cuts, sores, ulcers or boils, reduce pain and inflammation, and to relieve stings. Interestingly, some recent chemical analyses of these leaves show they do indeed have a therapeutic effect; being antiseptic, anti-inflammatory and antihistaminic.

Along some beach crests grassy, spinifex, patches grade into coastal shrubland that may be dominated by the pink-flowering fenzlia, *Fenzlia obtusa* (**left above**). Clumps of stately pandanus trees (**page 7, below**, & see page 16) and stands of willowy casuarinas, or she-oak trees, are also a familiar site along beach crests. Spiky casuarina cones and woody remains of the pineapple-like pandanus fruits contribute to strandline flotsam along with many other drift seeds and fruits, as do a great variety of dead shells and corals. Such areas are favourite nesting sites for birds such as Red-capped Dotterels and Beach Thick-knees (see page 42).

Coastal foredune sand is usually quite shelly but further inland the older dunes consist of deep soft fine siliceous sand. Extensive fields of well established older sand dunes dominate the landscape along the east coast of the Peninsula from Cape Bedford to Lookout Point, from the Olive River (**opposite below**) to Cape Grenville, and near Orford Ness. The dune crests may be fifteen to twenty metres high, although at White Point near Shelburne Bay (**left**) some may be as high as eighty metres. These dunefields are aligned in a southeast-northwest direction and are constantly on the move. The 'nose' of a dune, and less frequently its trailing arms, has active areas of advancing sand that continuously move forward in a northwest direction. Shallow freshwater 'window' lakes may form behind the trailing arms. These mature dunes are often well vegetated with heathland, woodland or even vine forest, which in exposed areas may be quite stunted.

Mangroves and Wetlands

Mangrove trees grow in intertidal areas and play an important role in stabilising coasts and estuaries, reclaiming land margins, preventing coastal erosion and acting as nurseries for many economically important crustaceans, molluscs and fish. On the Peninsula they occur in the larger sheltered bays along the east coast and along the north-west coast. By far the greatest stand of mangroves, not only on Cape York but in Australia (about 200 square kilometres), occurs in high rainfall areas around the Kennedy Inlet and Escape River in Newcastle Bay. The trees here may be as tall as 15 metres, and the forests are diverse with thirty three of Queensland's thirty eight mangrove species occurring. The most common mangroves are species of *Rhizophora* (**opposite above**) and *Bruguiera* and, in some areas, they form the bulk of the forest.

The splendid Mangrove Palm, *Nypa fruticans* (**right**), discovered in Australia in 1880, occurs sporadically along Australia's north-eastern and northern coasts, where it is locally abundant around margins of sheltered bays and along estuaries of coastal rivers. It can be seen along the Pascoe River in the Iron Range National Park. Nypa pollen is sticky and pollination may occur via the many insects that visit its flowers. Indeed, many insects such as Weaver Ants and Fireflies are important pollinators of mangrove flowers. Many animals can be seen in mangrove forests of the Peninsula including the Estaurine Crocodile (see page 29), Mangrove Monitor (see page 31) and the Great-billed Heron (see page 37).

Mangroves fringe river estuaries, tidal inlets and creeks of the vast saltflats and marine plains which occur in the low lying flatter areas of the south-west coast in the Carpentaria Basin and the southern end of Princess Charlotte Bay on the east coast of the Laura Basin (see page 6). The flats and plains may extend 30 kilometres inland and are dissected by many large river systems which, during the dry season, form an intricate network of watercourses. After the heavy wet season rains, however, they change dramatically – into vast, swampy, flood-plains. These areas, apart from some grassland (see page 13), are mostly devoid of vegetation as few plants can survive such harsh extreme climatic conditions. The elegant palm, *Corphya elata*, is an exception and isolated trees, or groves, are a characteristic feature on an otherwise flat monotonous landscape (**right**). A palm grove may represent all stages of growth – from seedlings and mature flowering or fruiting palms to those rotting away – for after fruiting just once in its lifetime the palm dies.

Tidal flats, floodplains, rivers and creeks, swamps, billabongs, waterholes, and seasonal and perennial lakes support an immense wealth of animal life, particularly waterbirds (see pages 36-39). The most widespread and significant wetland areas on the Peninsula occur between Aurukun and the Mitchell River, and in the Lakefield National Park. Python Lagoon (**opposite below**) is one of many lily-clad lakes in the park. Visitors to these wetland havens should take care not to disturb water birds. Beware also of crocodiles sunning themselves on muddy banks or lying in wait near the waters edge, ready to snap up unsuspecting prey that comes their way (see page 29).

River Systems

Most of the major river systems – the Jardine, Ducie, Wenlock, Embley, Hey, Archer, Edward, Alice, Mitchell, Palmer – rise on the eastern side of the Peninsula, west of the Great Dividing Range, and flow into the Gulf of Carpentaria. On the east coast are the Escape, Olive, Pascoe, Claudie, Lockhart, and Nesbit Rivers. Mangrove forests fringe many rivers near the coast, but further inland strips of woodland or vine forests dominate their banks. Stands of tall vine 'gallery' forests (see page 20) are a main feature of river banks in the Archer Bend and Mitchell and Alice Rivers National Parks.

The mighty Jardine River and its far-stretching catchment area of some 2500 square kilometres, often referred to as a 'wet desert', is one of the most impressive networks of watercourses on the Peninsula. The Jardine is the largest perennial river in Queensland. Its tributaries may be wide and fast flowing with picturesque waterfalls such as Twin Falls (**right**) or smaller, meandering, slow-moving backwaters such as Eliot Creek (**below**).

A large number of plants of prey flourish in this area. The pitcher plant, *Nepenthes mirabilis*, occurs along creek banks (**below**) and is also found in heathlands (**opposite above**). The ends of the leaves of this plant are modified into large, hollow, fluid-filled pitchers capped by a lid to keep out the rain. Unsuspecting insects, such as ants, climb along the ladder-like outer row of bristles to the slippery pitcher's rim, only to topple inside where they are then digested by the plant's enzymes within the fluid.

Heathlands and Grasslands

There are two main types of heath communities – open and closed. Open heath consists of low open areas of shrubs, less than one and a half metres tall, that grow on poorly-drained waterlogged soils. This swampy 'dwarf' heathland is dominated by the Cape York Heath Plant, as well as pitcher plants (**opposite below**), sundews and other plants of prey. Visitors to Iron Range drive through this type of heath as they appraoch Tozer's Gap (**left**).

Closed heath is denser, occurs on deeper better-drained soils, and has a canopy at about two metres with some emergent shrubs being four metres fall. Common plants include the orange-flowering Fern-leaved Grevillea, as well as other grevillea species, banksias, leptospermums and fenzlias (see page 9). Closed heath also occurs near Tozer's Gap, and on the east side of the Iron Range on the road to Portland Roads, and in upland areas near Mt. Tozer.

There are a number of grassland communities on the Peninsula, each community being dominated by different species of grass. One such community is characteristic of high rainfall areas and occurs in the lowland and hilly country, usually adjacent to vine forests, from Iron Range southwards towards Coen; and in the hilly country to the north-west of Cooktown. Grasses in this area are dense and may be as tall as two metres. These grasslands are quite distinct from those of the low-lying marine plains (see page 10) or beneath melaleuca and eucalypt woodlands or open-forests (see page 19). An extensive area of grassland occurs near Silver Plains (**below**).

Woodlands and Open-forests

Woodlands and open-forests cover by far the largest area of land on the Peninsula. Bandicoots, wallabies, wallaroos, kangaroos and dingoes flourish within these habitats. Tree hollows provide shelter for lizards, monitors, snakes and their prey; and possums retreat to them in the day, and may feed upon tree sap at night. Blossoms of eucalypts, melaleucas, acacias, and grevilleas, are a nectar-rich food source for butterflies, honeyeaters, lorikeets and flying-foxes.

Open-forests have a much denser canopy coverage (30-70%) than do woodlands (10-30%) and some woodlands are even more open with a sparser canopy coverage. Most woodland and open-forest trees are between ten to thirty metres tall, although some may be taller. In rugged sandstone country or on exposed dunefields trees may be more stunted and less than ten metres tall. Two major plant communities, both familiar to Australians as they occur elsewhere, dominate woodlands and open-forests; the *Melaleuca* paperbarks and the *Eucalyptus* stringybarks, bloodwoods, ironbarks and gum trees.

The Broad-leaved Tea Tree, *Melaleuca viridiflora*, is one of the most common paperbark species on the Peninsula. It prefers moister soils and flourishes in swampy woodland areas. Although its 'bottle-brush' flowers are usually cream or greenish yellow they may be pink or deep blood-red (**opposite**). The open branches of this paperbark, and its light leafy canopy, allow sunlight to reach all parts of the tree; providing an ideal situation for the growth of many epiphytic orchids, button plants and ant plants (see page 16).

The Tea Tree Orchid, *Dendrobium canaliculatum*, grows almost exclusively on the Broad-leaved Tea Tree. Its most common flower colour is a striking mixture of white, yellow and purple (**left above**) although another variety on the Peninsula has brown flowers. The Black Orchid, *Cymbidium canaliculatum* (**left**) is epiphytic mainly on eucalypts. Its flowers vary from light speckled brown through to a deep brownish-red colour – but not nearly as black as its common name implies. Both orchid species have swollen stems and thickened leaves to assist in moisture storage, which is an important adaptation for orchids that live in these drier habitats. Tea trees and these orchids are of great value indeed to Aboriginal people. The bark of the Broad-leaved Tea Tree is used for fire-tinder, shelters and bedding, and wrapping up food or corpses, and its trunk is used for building canoes. The fleshy stem bases of the Tea Tree Orchid are baked and eaten, and juices from them used to treat burns and wounds; and juices from the crushed stems of the Black Orchid are useful as a fixative for ochres used in bark or rock painting.

Some 110 species of orchids have been recorded on the Peninsula and thirteen of these are unique, or endemic. Other species also occur elsewhere in the Australian tropics, and some of them are found in New Guinea. The greatest density and diversity of orchid species thrives in damper habitats, such as vine forests (see page 20). Iron Range National Park is one the richest areas for orchid lovers. This is the heart of orchid country on the Peninsula and some sixty-six species occur there. The Jardine River, Lakefield, Archer Bend and Rockeby National Parks are also orchid-rich. Sadly, due to illegal collecting, some orchids are rare, even within National Parks.

The strange-looking epiphytic ant-plants (**right**) are a familiar and characteristic sight in the woodlands on the Peninsula; although they also occur in mangroves and vine forests. Trunks of melaleucas are a favourite site for ant-plant growth and, as shown in the picture, one tree may host several plants. Ant-plants, belonging to genera *Hydnophytum* and *Myrmecodia*, have large bulbous stems that are penetrated by an intricate system of hollow galleries, somewhat like the inside of a termite mound. Several species of tiny ants reside within this intricate network, giving the plant its common name.

Ants are not the only residents the plant hosts. The larvae of the Apollo Jewel Butterfly (see page 25) live within the ant galleries of the plant *Myrmecodia beccarii* where they have an extraordinary relationship with both plant and ants. By day the butterfly larvae feed upon the fleshy interior of the stem, and at night emerge to feed upon its leaves. Usually there is only one larva in each plant and just before it pupates it cuts a small circular exit hole. The myriads of ants do not harm the butterfly larva because it produces a fluid from special glands to the liking of the ants. Thus, the plant gains protection from the ants, the ants from the plants, the butterfly from both, and the ants gain advantage from the butterfly larva! The adult butterfly emerges through the exit hole and, like most jewel butterflies (see page 25), is quite exquisite.

A much more beautiful plant is the Cape York Lily, *Curcuma australasica* (**right below**), which grows mainly in sunny patches of open-forests. During the dry season the plant is dormant but as soon as it rains the single flower spike and large leaves emerge from the rhizome. The terminal flower spike, up to thirty centimetres tall, bears bright pinkish, papery, bracts that enclose yellow flowers. Like the ant-plant, this lily attracts insect associations. The axils of its inflorescence hold water, where many mosquito species breed. This is one of the few Australian examples of mosquitoes breeding in the inflorescence of a plant. In the South American bromeliads innumerable insect associations occur. The common name of this plant is a misnomer for it also occurs elsewehere in northern Australia and in New Guinea and is not a lily but belongs to the spice family, which includes ginger, turmeric and cardamom plants! Its rhizomes are roasted and eaten by aborigines.

Acacias, grevilleas, banksias, kapok (see page 46), fan and fishtail palms, cycads, grass trees (see page 19) and pandanus are all common plants of woodlands and open-forests on Cape York Peninsula. Many species of pandanus grow in this region where they occupy many habitats, including beach crests, heaths, vine forests and freshwater swamps and creeks in melaleuca woodland (**opposite**). Pandanus trees, or screw-pines as they are often called on account of the spiral arrangement of their prickly sword-like leaves around the stem, have aerial roots which may serve as stilt-roots or prop-roots to support them. They produce hard, often brightly-coloured pineapple-size red, orange or yellow fruits. The fruit is made up of fleshy, fibrous segments each containing a very edible kernel – a favourite food of the magnificant Palm Cockatoo (see page 45) and the handsome Black-footed Tree-rat (see page 68).

Eucalypt woodlands and open-forests are by far the most distinctive and common plant communities on the Peninsula. Eucalypt trees (**opposite**) occur on deeper sandy or earthy soils where they can seek moisture from great depths. The dominant species of eucalypt is the Stringybark, *Eucalyptus tetrodonta*, and it forms the most common vegetation community on the Peninsula (see page 2). Eucalypt woodlands with dense grassy ground cover, referred to as savannah woodlands, occur in central north-eastern areas and form one of the few areas of better natural grazing lands.

Fires, whether naturally occurring through lightning strikes or lit by pastoralists (see page 2), periodically sweep across large tracts of land. Eucalypts and many other plants of drier habitats such as grass trees, *Xanthorrhoea* species, have evolved adaptations to survive fires and recover quickly. Interestingly, grass trees acquired their other name of 'black-boys' because their fire-blackened trunks topped by a mop of tufted foliage resembled a stylised portrait of dark-skinned youth (**left**).

Eucalypt and grass trees are of great value to Aborigines, although much less so now than previously. Eucalypt bark is used in the making of shelters canoes, utensils and baskets; its wood is carved to make spears, digging tools, and artefacts such as didgeridoos; and its fragrant leaves are made into poultices to relieve aches and pains. The soft white bases of young shoots and leaves of grass trees are eaten raw; their large inflorescence soaked to produce a sweet drink; their light-weight flower spike used in the making of spears; and their resin is extracted and used as an adhesive in the making of tools.

Termite mounds are also of value. Parts of them are prepared and used medicinally as cures for diarrhoea, constipation, goitre, bronchitis and other ailments; and smoke from burning pieces of mounds is an effective mosquito repellent.

The profusion of vast termite mounds (front cover, pages ii, 5, and **left**) in the Peninsula woodlands and open-forests is undoubtedly one of the most outstanding and striking features of the landscape. They also occur in grasslands, heathlands and vine forests. The size and shape of termitaria vary according to the species of termite that build them. Some are small, low and domed; some are tall columns up to two metres or more in height; whilst others are wedge-shaped 'magnetic' mounds in which the long axis is orientated on a north-south line. Mound colour varies from sandy-grey (page ii) to a deep rich orange colour (page 5 and **left**) depending upon the colour of the soil used in their construction. Most termitaria are built on the ground but some are arboreal, attached to tree trunks.

The outer case of the termitarium is hard but within the material is softer and consists of an intricate maze of galleries and chambers. These contain termite eggs, nypmhs, and adult soldiers, workers and a royal pair. Termites feed on decaying wood, grass, fungi, dead leaves, bark, humus and even dung! Beetles and other invertebrates thrive within termite mounds, where there is a plentiful food supply of termite eggs and young. Birds such as the Golden-shouldered Parrot (see page 47), and Yellow-billed (see page 49) and Buff-breasted Paradise Kingfishers (see page 50) excavate active termite mounds to nest in.

Vine Forests

Australia's tropical rainforests occur in two main regions of coastal north-east Queensland; those of the Atherton Region of the wet tropics, that extend from just south of Cooktown to Paluma on the Seaview Range just north of Townsville, and those of Cape York Peninsula. These two regions are separated by a dry corridor from Cooktown northwards to just south of the McIlwraith Range. The wet and dry seasons north of Cooktown are more pronounced than those further south. The rainforests of the Peninsula are less diverse than those of the Atherton Region, have many species of deciduous trees, and are referred to as vine forests. Vine forests are classified as closed forests because, unlike the more open-forests and woodlands, they have a dense canopy cover of more than seventy percent. Most vine forests have trees at least thirty metres tall, with emergents of up to forty five metres, but in some drier areas of the Peninsula trees may be as low as ten metres and form scrubby vine thickets.

Large areas of vine forest occur near Bamaga, Lockerbie and at the head of the Jardine River, and at the Iron and McIlwraith Ranges. Smaller pockets are found in several other areas, particularly along creek and river banks where they are referred to as 'gallery' vine forests. Emergent Hoop Pines are a feature of the higher slopes of the McIlwraith Range vine forests whereas at Iron Range it is the emergent cluster fig trees that are characteristic. The ripe fruit of cluster figs are a favourite food of the Double-eyed Fig-Parrot (**right above** & see page 48). Some areas of the vine forest, such as can be seen at Rocky River in the McIlwraith Range (**right below**), are quite open and easy to walk through whilst others, particularly in wetter areas near creeks such as the West Claudie at Iron Range (**opposite**), are dense and quite impenetrable.

Vine forests support a rich diversity of mosses, ferns, orchids, gingers, palms, pandanus trees, lawyer vines, woody vines and robust lianes, and provide shelter and rich food resources for an incredible diversity of wildlife. Many species are unique, or endemic, to these forests and do not occur anywhere else on earth. Three species of frogs have only been found at McIlwraith Range (see page 26) and the Cinnamon Antechinus occurs only on the McIlwraith Range northwards to Iron Range (see page 63). Many of the species are restricted to these vine forests within Australia but also occur in New Guinea, where they are often more widespread and abundant. Such species include the Green Python (see page 33), the Palm Cockatoo (see page 45), the Eclectus Parrot (see page 48), Yellow-billed Kingfisher (see page 49) and the Spotted and Grey Cuscuses (see page 64). The distributional range of some species that also occur in New Guinea, such as the Southern Cassowary (see page 36) and the Striped Possum (see page 63), extends south of Cape York Peninsula to the Atherton Region. So close are the ties between New Guinea and Australia that a few species including the Torresian Imperial Pigeon (see page 44) and the Buff-breasted Paradise Kingfisher (see page 50) winter in New Guinea but migrate to tropical forests of north-eastern Queensland to breed. It is no wonder that some refer to the vine forests of the Peninsula as 'Australia's Little New Guinea'.

BUTTERFLIES

Butterflies reach their greatest species diversity in the tropics. The most important resource for butterflies is their larval food plant and for most that means foliage, flowers or fruits of living plants. The abundance and diversity of this resource helps account for the numbers of butterflies evident in northern tropical Australia. Of all the approximately 385 known Australian species about 300 occur in the tropics and of these some 225 occur on Cape York Peninsula. Of these approximately forty are peculiar to the Peninsula on continental Australia but (save two) also occur in New Guinea and islands.

All six butterfly families are represented on the Peninsula: the Hesperiidae, a group of mainly tropical species collectively known as skippers; the Papilionidae which includes the large and colourful triangles, swordtails, swallowtails and birdwings; the Pieridae, a family of almost entirely tropical white and yellow butterflies; the Nymphalidae, a large and diverse group that includes lacewings, ringlets, wanderers, tigers; the Lycaenidae, the largest Australian family, which includes small blues and spectacular jewels; and the Libytheidae, the smallest Australian family, consisting of one species – the Australian Beak.

Orange Dart
Suniana sunias

This flighty skipper (**right above**) may be seen wherever a sward of dense green grass is growing, especially in wet areas. The males will rest on blades of grass and aggressively defend their patch by flying rapidly after any passing butterfly before returning to their perch. Females seek out a variety of grasses on which to lay their eggs. The long slim larvae, or caterpillars, are green with a black head, and they construct tubular shelters by rolling a blade of grass. They emerge to feed on other parts of the same blade of grass, eventually leaving nothing but the midrib and their shelter. At this stage they move to another blade and new shelter.

Some of Australia's most attractive skippers occur on the Peninsula including the Peacock Awl, the Banded Red-eye, the Black and White Flat, and the Black and White Swift.

Fivebar Swordtail
Graphium aristeus

The forewing surface of this butterfly (**right**) has five distinct bars along its leading edge. The larval stages were first observed in deciduous vine thickets on the Peninsula in January 1988. It flies only in summer and the pupae go into diapause (arrested development, a kind of hibernation) for the rest of the year. The pupae may be found on the food plant or under rocks at its base. It is thought that adults emerge from pupae in reponse to major summer rain and at this time may be locally abundant. Males are known to 'hilltop' that is they congregate on hill summits and establish territory, and aggressively defend perches and adjacent terrain from other males. Eventually a female will arrive and be located by a male; after mating the females leave the hilltop but males stay for the remainder of their lives. The closely related Fourbar Swordtail also occurs on the Peninsula and is associated with vine thickets.

Red-bodied Swallowtail
Pachliopta polydorus

This attractive butterfly (**left**) is one of the commonest species at Iron Range along tracks or near the edges of forest patches. The larvae feed on *Aristolochia* vines, plants also used as food plants by the somewhat similar looking Big Greasy Butterfly; and by Birdwing Butterflies (see below). The egg is laid singly on a leaf and the young larva eats the eggshell before feeding on the food plant. The caterpillar is brown with scattered fleshy tubercles of red or yellowish colour. The pupa is very distinctly lobed, quite unlike any other Australian species. They usually pupate under a leaf but have been found beneath rocks amongst vine thickets on Mt. White, near Coen. The adults are slow flyers and fed commonly at flowers growing at forest margins.

Several other papilionid butterflies occur on the Peninsula including one of the most spectacular of all butterflies the blue Ulysses Butterfly, which has become a symbol of tourism throughout north Queensland, and the less colourful Capaneus Butterfly which is notably abundant in vine thickets.

Birdwing Butterfly
Ornithoptera priamus

This species is strongly dimorphic; the males being richly coloured in green, gold and black (**left**) whereas the larger females, with a wing span of up to twenty centimetres across, are black and white with yellow markings on the hindwings. There can be few sights as spectacular as a soaring Birdwing Butterfly gliding amongst the canopy or sweeping down to investigate a flower. Writing in 1856, the great naturalist Alfred Wallace described his joy at seeing a birdwing during his sojourn in the Malay Archipelago. To him *Ornithoptera* were the 'largest most perfect and beautiful of butterflies'. Many people today would share this view, and in Papua New Guinea birdwings are carefully farmed.

These magnificant butterflies have been observed feeding in the Iron Range vine thickets on the massive yellow blossoms of the Golden Bouquet Tree, sharing the nectar with a Graceful Honeyeater (see page 56), completely dwarfed by the butterflies! Males sometimes set up territory near the larval food plant, a vigorous large-leaved vine, *Aristolochia tagala*, and in the early morning patrol around its base in search of freshly emerging females. These may be mated before their wings are dry and it is not unusual to see two or three males trying to copulate with a single female.

This species has been divided into fourteen subspecies; three occur on Cape York Peninsula and a fourth (**left**) in north-eastern Australia from Cooktown to Mackay. They differ slightly in size and wing markings. Other subspecies are found in the Moluccas, New Guinea, the Kai and Aru islands, the Bismarck Archipelago and the Solomon Islands.

Hamadryad
Tellervo zoilus

This attractive butterfly (**left**) is frequently seen fluttering and gliding in and out of vine forest openings. Its yellow eyes are distinctive. Its larval food-plant is a large-leaved vine, *Parsonsia* species. The larva is colourful with a pair of black fleshy filaments rising from bright yellow bases immediately behind the head. The body is narrowly banded black and white with a pair of yellow patches at the rear.

Northern Jezabel
Delias argenthona

This species occurs in eucalypt woodland. The scarlet markings underneath stand out in contrast to the white upper surface (**opposite above**). The female has more yellow and even her upper surface is tinged with yellow. Eggs are laid in clusters on a fresh leaf of mistletoe and the larvae feed together along the edges of the leaves. The Orange Jezabel, so-called because of the orange-yellow of the upper wings, is endemic to the Peninsula.

Common Australian Crow
Euploea core

This familiar butterfly looks like other crow butterflies but has many more white markings. The larvae are quite colourful with narrow black and white bands and four pairs of fleshy filaments. The pupa is remarkable for it turns a brilliant shining silver, or gold, seemingly metallic, with a few markings. It is suspended beneath a leaf and just before the adult emerges becomes black and white as the adult colours show through the transparent pupal skin. In winter months many Australian crows form large clustered aggregations (**opposite below**), usually in sheltered gullies and creeks. It is easy to confuse this species with the similar looking, but not so extensively marked, Eichhorn's Crow which also congregates along streams and rivers during the dry season.

Fiery Jewel
Hypochrysops ignitus

Fiery Jewels (**left**) occur in colonies which require two essential ingredients – one of a few species of ants must be present, together with an appropriate plant species. The ants build nests around the base of the food plants – usually re-growth or young plants, often wattles but also Cocky Apple and Red Ash. A female will usually lay a small cluster of eggs and the larvae will remain together during their life. Larvae shelter below the ground in the ant byres or sometimes in the abandoned cocoons of large moths or even curled leaves. They are always attended by numerous ants. The male Fiery Jewel occurs commonly on hill tops in open-forests where it usually perches on a leaf of a gum or wattle tree and from where it challenges other butterflies. The upperwing of the adult is purple in the male and pale blue in the female. In common with other jewels the underside is most spectacular.

25

FROGS

About thirty of Australia's 190 frog species occur on the Peninsula; and all four frog families in Australia are represented there. Almost two thirds of those species on the Peninsula are tree frogs of the family Hylidae, mostly belonging to the genus *Litoria*. The Marbled Frog, Ornate Burrowing Frog and the Northern Banjo Frog, members of the family Myobatrachidae, are commonly encountered on the Peninsula but are also found further south, predominantly in other tropical areas. Of the truly tropical family of Microhylidae only one species, *Sphenophryne robusta*, occurs through-out northern Cape York Peninsula, as well as occurring in Arnhemland and in the Atherton Region. The Wood Frog (**right below**) is the only 'true' frog in Australia, being one of 610 species in the cosmopolitan family Ranidae. The Wood Frog and the introduced Cane Toad are both found in this region. One hylid tree frog, *Litoria longirostris*, and two species of microhylids of the genus *Cophixalus* are unique, or endemic, to the McIlwraith Range.

Giant Tree Frog
Litoria infrafrenata

This is the largest tree frog on earth (**right above**) averaging ten centimetres long from snout to vent (cloaca). Some individuals reach fourteen centimetres. It is confined to the rainforests of Cape York Peninsula and south to Ingham, and is also found in eastern Indonesia and New Guinea and surrounding islands. Giant Tree Frogs are commonly seen at night in vine forests at Iron Range when they emerge from their daytime retreats on warm humid evenings, especially after rain, to hunt insects. The male mating call sounds similar to a dog bark. When molested frogs may produce a loud distressing miaowing, like the sound of a cat.

The Giant Tree Frog is identified from its close relative the Green Tree Frog by its conspicuous white lower lip. Another, smaller green tree frog found on the Peninsula is the Dainty Green Tree Frog. Interestingly, the Cape York form of it has a distinct bluish tinge along the hind side of its thighs whereas elsewhere within its eastern Queeensland range this is a reddish-brown.

Many other *Litoria* species are found in this region in swampy areas, amongst vegetation around temporary pools, lagoons, and creek banks, leaf axils of pandanus trees and other moist situations. Some of the more common ones include the Striped Burrowing Frog, the Northern Dwarf Tree Frog, the Dwarf Rocket Frog, the Rocket Frog and the Desert Tree Frog.

Wood Frog
Rana daemeli

The Wood Frog (**right**) is restricted to northern and eastern Cape York Peninsula and south to Ingham. It is a terrestrial and semi-aquatic frog. It grows to an average length of eight centimetres, and is an efficient ground predator commonly encountered close to streams and permanent pools and lagoons in vine forests, melaleuca swamps, and other dense vegetation. The characteristic call is a reedy duck-like quacking series of notes repeated up to about eight times.

REPTILES

About 160 of some 690 species of reptiles in Australia have been recorded on Cape York Peninsula, and all major reptile groups occur here. It is difficult to provide a precise number of species for this area as new species, particularly smaller skinks, are still being discovered and described. Both species of crocodiles (family Crocodylidae) are predominantly tropical and both are common residents of rivers and lagoons on the Peninsula (see page 29). Marine turtles and terrestrial tortoises constitute the order Chelonia; all Australian turtle species occur in seas around the Cape, and seven of the Australian seventeen tortoises are found on the Peninsula.

The approximately 500 Australian lizards belong to five of the world's sixteen lizard families, of the order Squamata and suborder Sauria. The lizard fauna of Cape York Peninsula comprises of some eighteen gecko species (family Gekkonidae), three legless lizards (family Pygopodidae), seven dragon lizards (family Agamidae), eight monitors or goannas (family Varanidae) and thirty five or so skinks (family Scincidae); at least one gecko and seven skink species are peculiar, or endemic. Snakes belong to the order Squamata, together with the lizards, and constitute the suborder Serpentes. Of the approximately 132 Australian snakes (excluding sea snakes) some forty five occur on the Peninsula.

Ring-tailed Gecko
Cyrtodactylus louisiadensis

One of the most spectacular geckoes is undoubtedly the Ring-tailed Gecko (**left above**). Ring-tailed Geckoes are commonly to be seen moving about on rocks and large boulders at night, quickly retiring to crevices and caves when disturbed, but may also be found perched low down on tree trunks or woody debris. This gecko and the Northern Leaf-tailed Gecko are the largest of Australian geckoes, with an average adult length of sixteen centimetres, some individuals attaining a maximum twenty five centimetres, snout to vent length. The Northern Leaf-tailed Gecko and the slightly smaller Giant Tree Gecko which is endemic to the Cape, occur mostly in vine forests. Other geckoes found on the Peninsula such as Bynoe's Gecko and the Northern Velvet Gecko favour more arid environments.

Jewel Skink
Carlia jarnoldae

Male Jewel Skinks (**left**) in breeding colouration are as spectacular as any of the small skinks. Females are different, being generally dark brown above with scattered black and white flecks, and a paler coppery-brown head. A clear white line runs from the lips down the entire length of each side of both sexes to the hind leg, which is contrasted above by a broad black stripe, and below by a less clear blackish line. The sexual difference is noteworthy because the sexes of the vast majority of skinks are nearly identical. This insectivorous skink is only four centimetres long.

Many skink species occur on the Peninsula on rocky outcrops, in sandstone areas, and amongst litter about the bases of trees, logs and stones in heathland, woodlands, open forests and vine forests. One of the largest and heaviest is the Major Skink which may be eighteen centimetres snout to vent.

New Guinea Snake-necked Tortoise
Chelodina novaeguineae

This tortoise (**opposite above**), with an adult shell length of about thirty centimetres, is so named because it was first discovered in New Guinea. The neck is very long, the photographed individual having its neck folded to the side and beneath its shell. It frequents rivers, billabongs, swamps and pools and feeds on aquatic animals including molluscs, smaller fish, crustaceans and amphibians. As much of its water habitat dries annually, during the dry season, this tortoise then remains underground, in mud, in a metabolically suspended state called aestivation.

Estuarine Crocodile
Crocodylus porosus

This awesome crocodile (**left**) may attain a total length of over seven metres, but few individuals have been found larger than five metres long. It is much stouter than the Freshwater Crocodile (**opposite below**) which also has a much narrower, relatively longer snout. Estuarine Crocodiles of great length are creatures of considerable girth and weight. They inhabit coastal estuaries and swamps, but also dwell in rivers, billabongs and lagoons anywhere on the Peninsula, often many kilometres inland, reached via river systems during periods of flood.

The Estuarine Crocodile is a very delicate animal when it comes to its nesting habits. Females ready to lay their eggs scrape together a substantial mound of debris, vegetation and soil on a river or billabong bank with their feet, tail, and even the sides of the body. Once the nest is complete the female lays across the apex (**left**) and digs an egg chamber with her hind legs. She then raises her hind quarters slightly to deposit her thirty to eighty white hard-shelled eggs and then covers them carefully with sensitive movements of her legs. On completion she retires to adjacent water or wallow to await egg hatching. From here she will vigorously defend the nest and eggs from any disturbance. She returns to the nest when the young can be heard giving their little yelping calls from the egg, to actually carry the hatchlings to the water in her powerful toothy mouth!

Freshwater Crocodile
Crocodylus johnstoni

The Freshwater Crocodile (**opposite below**) may attain an adult total length of three metres. It is common in upstream freshwater rivers, billabongs and lagoons of the Peninsula, but also occurs in tidal areas of some rivers. It feeds mostly at night, but is active during the day and may be seen basking in the sun or swimming. Its diet includes small mammals, birds, reptiles, amphibians, fish, crustaceans, insects and even spiders, as well as smaller individuals of its own kind. Breeding takes place during the early spring when females lay aproximately fifteen to twenty five hard-shelled eggs in a sandy riverbank, where they will hatch some three months later before the wet season rains cause flooding of the nest sites.

Frilled Lizard
Chlamydosaurus kingii

This lizard (**right**) qualifies for the descriptive word bizzare, as there is no other species on earth with a frill, like this. The frill can be colourful, and when erected areas of yellow, orange, pink or rust-red may be revealed. Its remarkable defensive posture with frill fully erect and mouth wide open may be made the more effective by a lashing out at the intruder with the large wiry tail. This is followed by its amusing bipedal striding escape-run to a tree, when its bluff has failed. It is our largest agamid lizard, with a length of twenty two centimetres, but with an extremely long tail that may result in an overall length of eighty five centimetres. Frilled Lizards are diurnal and eat larger insects, spiders and smaller mammals.

Gould's Goanna
Varanus gouldii

Gould's Goanna (**below**) is a ground dwelling monitor of woodlands, open-forests and more arid environments, where it rests in hollow logs, ground burrows of other animals, or holes excavated by itself. The photograph shows an individual of the lighter yellow and black form, but others can be much darker to almost black above. Large individuals may grow to over one and a half metres and weigh more than seven kilograms. Gould's Goanna has powerful strong limbs equipped with sharp claws for rock and tree climbing or hole-digging. It eats carrion, mammals, birds, reptiles and insects.

Mangrove Monitor
Varanus indicus

This (**left**) is an exclusively tropical goanna, confined to coastal mangrove and rainforest vegetation of the extreme northern tropics, including Torres Strait Islands. It is a solidly built monitor growing to an average of about a metre and a maximum of almost two metres total length, that closely associates with mangrove and lowland rainforest creeks. It is a competent swimmer, strongly propelling itself with long laterally flattened tail. Foods include fish, crustaceans, insects, birds, mammals and amphibians and some reptiles, including hatchling crocodiles. It is sometimes mistaken for a crocodile because of its aquatic habits within crocodile habitats.

Merten's Water Monitor
Varanus mertensi

Merten's Water Monitor is another water-frequenting species (**below**) confined to tropical Australia, but is far less restricted than the Mangrove Monitor and may be found great distances from the coast. It commonly attains a total length of one metre, but does not grow to as large as the Mangrove Monitor. It feeds upon fish, frogs, reptiles, crustaceans, insects, carrion and doubtless much more. It takes to water when alarmed, like the previous species. The photograph shows the neck much inflated in aggressive posture.

Water Python
Liasis (fuscus) mackloti

The Water Python (**left**), as its name suggests, is most frequently encountered near river systems and wetland areas in the immediate vicinity of flowing or standing water. It likes to have the immediate availability of water to hunt and to escape into if alarmed, and may be found in burrows, among rocks or in hollow logs closeby. Foods of this nocturnal python include mammals, birds and reptiles including smaller young fresh-water crocodiles. The adult Water Python may be about two metres in length, but individuals may be up to three metres long. Up to eleven eggs have been recorded as laid by this python which the female, as in all Australian pythons, coils tightly around to protect and incubate.

Of the fifteen pythons (family Boidae) presently recognised in Australia, seven occur on the Peninsula – the four illustrated on these pages, and the Black-headed, Spotted and Carpet Pythons.

Green Python
Chondropython viridis

Confined to the vine forests of the Peninsula, and also found in New Guinea, this lovely python (**opposite above**) has remarkable juvenile colourations of bright yellow or a rich brick-red with delicate gold markings. Juvenile colouration is lost to adult green at about two years of age over a period of two days to two weeks, without a skin change. It hunts birds and mammals at night, or basks in sunlight, in trees, vines and epiphytic plants. Daylight may be spent in tree hollows or coiled among suitable sheltered vegetation such as epiphytic ferns. It does sometimes visit the ground to hunt or rest. Thirteen to twenty soft shelled eggs are laid by this python which may attain a total length of about two metres.

Amethystine Python
Morelia amethistina

This python (**opposite below**), named for the lovely amethystine-like iridescence that can usually be seen on its scales when available light permits, is Australia's largest and has been authentically recorded at eight and a half metres (28 feet) long. It preys upon a large range of mammals including fruit bats, possums, rats, pademelons and wallabies; and also eats birds. It inhabits mangroves and wetter habitats of woodlands and vine forests. Females lay a clutch of between ten to twenty eggs that form a cohesive clump.

Olive Python
Liasis olivaceus

The Olive Python (**left**) is superficially similar to the Water Python, but it grows to be a larger snake, attaining a maximum length of about four metres. Whilst predominantly tropical in distribution the Olive Python is absent from the eastern half of the Peninsula, being primarily adapted to slightly drier environments where it is especially fond of rocky areas and frequents rock crevices, caves and hollow logs. It prefers to be in the proximity of water where it feeds upon mammals, birds and the occasional reptile.

Brown Tree Snake
Boiga irregularis

The Brown Tree Snake is a member of the approximately 1,560 snake species of the world in the family Colubridae that are often collectively, but in some cases misleadingly, referred to as the harmless snakes. The Colubridae does in fact contain numerous rear-fanged venomous snakes, but because of their mostly milder poison and/or less sophisticated mechanisms for administering it they are not as dangerous to people as the front-fanged venomous snakes of the family Elapidae.

Brown Tree Snakes live throughout the northern Australian tropics and are commonly encountered on the Peninsula in various habitats such as woodlands and vine forests where they shelter in caves, rock or tree crevices and hollow logs. The one illustrated (**right**) was found coiled up in a tree hollow in vine forests at Iron Range. The colouration of the snake in the photograph is fairly typical of individuals of eastern Australia but in the north and north-west they are cream or whitish to reddish-brown with numerous and conspicuous bright red to red-brown cross bands. Characteristic of this snake are its long slender body with a conspicuously bulbous head with relatively huge staring eyes that have vertically slit, cat-like, pupils.

An average adult measures about one and a half metres, reaching a maximum length of about two metres. It is a nocturnal and arboreal snake, well adapted with large slit-pupil eyes, and agile body, and with appropriate belly scales to obtain purchase on tree bark. It is, whilst a rear-fanged venomous snake, harmless. When disturbed it performs a most impressive threat display by bending the neck and fore-body back into many loops, hissing, and often opening the mouth widely. If pressed closely it strikes and bites viciously. Its food consists of a wide range of small mammals, birds and their eggs and nestlings, and lizards. It is an egg-laying snake with clutches consisting of at least five to a dozen eggs.

Other colubrids common on the Peninsula include other tree snakes (see below), the Keelback or Freshwater Snake, Macleay's Water Snake and the Slaty-grey Snake.

Northern Tree Snake
Dendrelaphis calligastra

Both the Northern Tree Snake and the near-identical Common Tree Snake occur on the Peninsula. The Common Tree Snake is more widely distributed in Australia than this species which is confined to tropical east coast of Cape York Peninsula south to the Townsville region, where it appears to associate with vine forests, rainforests and other wetter forest habitats. The lovely and harmless Northern Tree Snake illustrated here (**right**) differs, however, from the Common in having relatively larger eyes and a blackish streak from the snout tip back along either side of the face, through the lower eye, onto the neck. It is a long thin and agile snake commonly seen above the ground climbing in trees, vines and about human dwellings in daylight. It is usually rich brown to olive above with yellow or creamish underparts often flecked with darker markings. It has been recorded feeding upon frogs and small lizards.

Papuan Black Whip Snake
Demansia papuensis

Australia is renowned for its large number of dangerously venomous snakes, belonging to the family Elapidae. Although these front-fanged snakes are referred to collectively as dangerous, most species lack sufficiently potent venom or delivery mechanisms to be a threat to people. The Papuan Black Whip Snake reaches nearly two metres long and whilst no death has been attributed to its bite it is possible a large individual might kill a small person of poor health. It should be treated with great respect, particularly in view of its great speed.

Like all six whip snakes of the genus *Demansia*, this is a long slender fast-moving snake with a relatively large eye (**left**). Note the smudged black spots atop the head of this snake. It is a black or very dark grey-brown above with a paler face, and the tail is also paler and brownish to reddish. Underparts are greyish. It is found in drier habitats on the Peninsula where it hunts skinks and other small vertebrates.

The closely related Black Whip Snake, the Yellow-faced Whip Snake and the Collared Whip Snake also occur on the Peninsula in drier habitats and in some areas of their range may occur together.

Taipan
Oxyuranus scutellatus

The Taipan is one of most dangerous snakes on earth and needs little introduction to most Australians, as it is an infamous snake despite its predominantly tropical distribution in Australia and New Guinea. Taipans grow large and inject substantial quantities of highly poisonous venom through long fangs, making them particularly dangerous. Prior to the manufacture of Taipan antivenom almost all people well bitten by it died.

The Taipan has a characteristic long and somewhat rectangular-shaped head (**left**). It may be uniform pale to dark brown, olive, coppery-red or black above but almost always has a pale whitish or cream face set off by a large and 'intelligent' pale eye. The belly is yellow to cream with irregular flecks and spots of orange. An average adult measures two metres, but some individuals have been recorded at about three metres long.

Taipans are found in woodlands, open-forests and other drier habitats where they are usually diurnal and crepuscular, but may be nocturnal in the early evenings on hot nights. They feed predominantly upon small mammals, especially mice and rats, but occasionally upon lizards and birds. Under normal wild conditions this snake is an alert, intelligent, nervous, retiring species that will avoid disturbance whenever possible. It is snakes that people suddenly surprise, corner, or attempt to catch or kill that inflict their terrible bite. This is of course a snake to be avoided and left well alone if seen. Other extremely dangerous elapid snakes to avoid on Cape York Peninsula include the Mulga or King Brown Snake, the Eastern or Common Brown Snake, and the Western Brown Snake or Gwardar.

BIRDS

Of the approximately 725 species of birds recorded in Australia and adjacent seas some 323, or forty five percent may be seen at least somewhere on Cape York Peninsula or its adjacent waters. Of this 323 species, which exclude uncommon or vagrant species, 218 are birds found widely in Australia, beyond the Peninsula. Eighty species are of very predominantly tropical distributions in Australia but are also found south of the tropics; and twenty three are only found on the Peninsula in Australia but also occur in New Guinea or other islands to the north. Only two species are truly unique, or endemic, to Cape York Peninsula; the Golden-shouldered Parrot (see page 47) and the White-streaked Honeyeater (see page 56).

As much of the Peninsula is woodland and open-forest, with most birds occurring in these habitats south of the region, it is inevitable that many bird-watchers seek out the New Guinea birds that are restricted to vine forests of the northern tip, the Iron Range area and McIlwraith Range. Birds such as the spectacular Palm Cockatoo, Eclectus Parrot, Red-cheeked Parrot, the Chestnut-breasted Cuckoo, Yellow-billed Kingfisher, Red-bellied Pitta, Northern Scrub-robin, Yellow-footed Flycatcher, White-faced Robin, Black-winged Monarch, Frilled Monarch, Tropical Scrubwren, Tawny-breasted Honeyeater, Green-backed Honeyeater, White-streaked Honeyeater, and the wonderful birds of paradise, the Magnificent Riflebird and the Trumpet Manucode, all attract an ever-increasing number of national and international bird-watchers to Australia's 'Little New Guinea' (see pages 45-61).

 ## Southern Cassowary
Casuarius casuarius

This huge flightless bird (**right above**) is a remnant of the avian past, a primitive living bird known as a ratite; as are the New Zealand Kiwis, Ostriches of Africa, Rheas of South America and our familiar Emu. The Southern Cassowary occurs in dense tropical rainforests from Paluma, just north of Townsville, to northern Cape York Peninsula and New Guinea. Heavy dense plumage, horny-looking casque atop the skull, and three to five odd large wire-like feather quills that extend from the vestigial wings, are believed to provide protection for the bird in its rainforest environment. As it runs quickly through the forest the head is lowered, casque upright, and plumage and wing quills are held out to brush aside impeding foliage. Other than their dense blue-black feathering adult cassowaries sport bright hues of red and blue bare skin about the head and neck with bare red neck wattles, doubtless as conspicuous social signals to their kind. Immature birds have brown feathering, lack a casque, and have paler, pinkish or yellowish, wattles.

Female cassowaries, which are larger than males, are promiscuous and lay eggs in several male egg scrapes (not a nest really) only to leave the male with the family duties of incubating the the huge one to five blue-green eggs and caring for the newly-hatched delightful brown and cream striped chicks (**right above**).

New Guinea is home to two other cassowary species, the large lowland Northern or Single-wattled Cassowary, and the Dwarf Cassowary of the highlands.

Black-necked Stork
Ephippiorhynchus asiaticus

This impressive bird (**opposite below**) is better known to most Australians as the Jabiru. It is one of seventeen stork species on earth and is the only Australian representative of that group of large and huge-billed birds. It builds an enormous bulky stick platform nest in dead or live trees and also in low shrubs or even on the ground; both male (black eyes) and female (yellow eyes) attend the eggs and nestlings. The Black-necked Stork is a bird of estuaries, mangroves, mudflats, swamplands, floodplains and other wetland habitats where it feeds upon fish, eels, frogs and other large aquatic animals.

The wetland areas of Cape York Peninsula (see page 10) are a haven for innumerable numbers of waterbird species including the Black-necked Stork, herons (see below), ibises, spoonbills, geese, pelicans, waterfowl, and cranes. They are, therefore, a paradise for bird watchers, naturalists and photographers; for they not only support some of the largest breeding populations in Australia but are also used by many migratory waterbirds.

Great-billed Heron
Ardea sumatrana

This very large dark grey-brown heron is shy and difficult to approach. It occurs along tidal mudflats and estuaries, mangrove-lined creeks and further inland along smaller forested creeks.

Of the fourteen herons commonly found within Australia this stately bird (**left above**) is one of the only two species restricted as a breeding species within the tropics, the other being the Pied Heron (below). All other Australian herons (including egrets, night-herons and bitterns) except two, the Little and Australian Bitterns, occur on the Peninsula and major breeding colonies of them can be seen in mangroves on the Love and Holroyd Rivers on the west coast.

Pied Heron
Ardea picata

Within its exclusively tropical range (excepting semi-vagrant records for southern South Australia) this bird (**left**) associates closely with coastal and subcoastal swamps, lakes and lagoons and may also be seen on river margins, mudflats and in mangrove areas. Some populations move to New Guinea and Indonesia during our dry season whilst others, perhaps the majority, remain here. Platform stick nests are built in live or dead trees, often in mangrove forests. Two to four eggs are laid. This lovely heron feeds upon aquatic animal life, mostly insects but also fish and amphibians.

Pied Herons breed colonially, often associated with other colonial nesting herons or ibises or cormorants. The Mitchell River delta is one location where this species is known to breed, but almost nothing is known of the breeding behaviour and biology of this photogenic bird.

Magpie Goose
Anseranus semipalmata

The black and white Magpie, or Pied, Goose (**right**) is given the great distinction of its own family! Its feet are only partly webbed and this is clearly an adaptation to the bird's way of life. It commonly perches in trees and often walks considerable distances. The bird is also noteworthy for the conspicuous bulbous knob on its crown, which is usually larger in males. Adult males have a greatly lengthened windpipe, that extends in a double coil down on to the breast muscle, beneath the skin, which enables them to produce a very loud honking.

Magpie Geese are common in swamplands, floodplains, wet grasslands and other wetland areas where they feed on the bulbs of spike-rush, sedges, grasses and seeds. Large nesting colonies of them can be seen around Aurukun, and they are also common in Lakefield National Park. They are often seen associated with Brolgas (**right**).

Brolga
Grus rubicundus

The Brolga (**right**) and the Sarus Crane (**opposite**) are two of the worlds fourteen species of crane; tall long-legged stately birds. The Brolga is a bird of shallow swamplands, flood plains, wetlands, grasslands and other wetter open areas, where it probes into mud with its dagger-like bill for sedge tubers. It also eats insects, such as grasshoppers. Brolgas may be seen in very large flocks, particularly when the dry season reduces wetlands and birds must congregate on limited areas of shallow water. Brolgas are well known for performing ritualised courtship display dances, during which birds leap about with extended wings whilst throwing the head back or bowing it down-ward, and kicking their long legs out and calling.

Sarus Crane
Grus antigone

As recently as 1966 small parties of Sarus Crane were first discovered in Australia amongst Brolgas near Burketown and Normanton, just south of the Peninsula. The Sarus Crane (**opposite**) is distinguished from the Brolga by its more extensive bare scarlet skin about head, throat upper neck.

Plumed Whistling Duck
Dendrocygna eytoni

This duck (**right**) and the closely related Diving Whistling Duck are common waterfowl of wetlands. Both are handsome long-legged and long-necked ducks which used to be referred to as tree ducks because, unlike most ducks, they perch in trees. The Diving Whistling Duck feeds in deeper lagoon water by diving. The Plumed Whistling Duck does not dive but may dabble whilst feeding.

Other species of waterfowl recorded from the wetlands of the Peninsula include the predominantly tropical White-headed Shelduck, the White Pygmy Goose, the Green Pygmy Goose and many other more widespread species.

Black Kite
Milvus migrans

Of Australia's twenty four raptors or 'diurnal birds of prey', only two, the Letter-winged Kite and the Grey Falcon, do not occur on Cape York Peninsula. Of the twenty two species that do occur there the Black Kite, together with the Whistling Kite, would be the most frequently seen and familiar.

The Black, or Fork-tailed, Kite (**right**) is a scavenger and a very well known one throughout its vast range of Europe, Asia, Africa, South East Asia to New Guinea and surrounding islands. It is a bird that has benefited much by human settlement, providing it with food and water in areas it would otherwise be unable to inhabit. Roads provide birds with an endless supply of carrion in the form of mammals, birds and insects killed by vehicles, and it is the masterful aerial manoeuvering of birds over road kills that attracts the layman's eye to this species. Fires, too, are much to Black Kites' great advantage. No sooner is a bush fire started that numbers of these birds appear, as if from nowhere, to snatch up insects and other prey injured, or escaping from, the flames and ashes. Rubbish tips are another novel foraging site for Black Kites, where tropical resident people are familiar with the sight of numbers of these birds perched in surrounding trees, awaiting the next arrival of those nice upright clothed creatures that throw away so much good food!

Rufous Owl
Ninox rufa

The Rufous Owl is Australia's second largest owl species, but many consider it the most outstanding because of its rich and fine markings. Spotlighting at night through the Iron Range vine forests and adjacent woodlands is a rewarding experience, for here it is possible to see many of our nocturnal birds – owls, frogmouths, owlet-nightjars and nightjars. It was during such a foray that we were lucky enough to encounter and photograph the Rufous Owl (**right**), one of the rarest and least known of Australia's nine owl species.

This impressive and ferocious owl occurs only within tropical Australia, from the Mackay area of Queensland northwards up the coastal zone to the tip of Cape York. Another population occupies Arnhemland of the Northern Territory and the Kimberley Region of Western Australia. Rufous Owls dwell in rainforests and other dense wet forests including melaleuca forests and sometimes mangroves. They are able to kill large birds, such as the Australian Brush-turkey (**opposite below**), and mammals such as flying foxes and possums.

The Papuan Frogmouth and the much rarer Marbled Frogmouth may also be spotlighted in this area. Frogmouths are closely related to owls but are members of a different family of birds and as such are quite different in many respects. Their feet are quite small and are weak, being adapted for perching only and are no use for capturing prey as are the powerful talons of owls. As their name implies, frogmouths have huge mouths, used to snap up large insects, frogs, lizards, mice and other small animals from the ground and vegetation.

Orange-footed Scrubfowl
Megapodius reinwardt

The Orange-footed Scrubfowl (**left**) is confined strictly to the tropics in Australia, but is widespread in New Guinea, Indonesia and the South Pacific islands. This bird and the Australian Brush-turkey (see below) and Malleefowl of arid southern Australia constitute the three Australian representatives of the family Megapodidae or mound-builders. These remarkable, large terrestrial birds are so named because the males of most species accumulate vast mounds of vegetation and sand by scratching with their large feet. These mounds are in fact incubator nests, in which females will lay their eggs for the male to subsequently care for, by maintaining the temperature and humidity within the mound at the optimum for egg incubation. This is done by the industrious bird adding or subtracting mound material to compensate for changes in climate.

The Scrubfowl is very vocal indeed, producing weird and wonderful extremely loud crows, cries and screams, often throughout the night. Birds become quite familiar about camp sites, if the human occupants are not too loud and rude in their activities. In the wet forested coastal areas of the Cape people are often awe-struck by the massive proportions of some nest mounds – which look as if a very large tipper truck has dropped a full load of mulch in the forest. A quick look at the surrounding forest floor, if scraped almost spotlessly clean of litter, indicates that the mound is actively in use.

Australian Brush-turkey
Alectura lathami

This is another megapode or mound builder (see above) that is more widespread and familiar to Australians, occurring southwards of Cape York Peninsula down eastern Queensland and north-east New South Wales to Sydney. Brush-turkeys live in a wide range of habitats on the Peninsula, from the landward edge of mangrove forests and in dense vine forests to the open and barren habitats of the centre of the Peninsula.

As in the Orange-footed Scrubfowl, males build large mounds in which females lay their eggs. These birds feed rather like domestic fowls, scraping away leaf litter with their feet and pecking at exposed foods. They are omnivorous, which is to say they eat both vegetable and animal foods. The tail of the Brush-turkey is remarkable in being held on a vertical axis, which it fans and closes during social encounters, possibly to indicate dominance or submissiveness. Unlike the far better known populations of birds south of the Peninsula, which have bright yellow wattle skin, the wattles of the northern birds are a delicate purple-mauve (**left**).

Australian Bustard
Ardeotis australis

This heavy and stately bird (**right**) was unfortunate enough to be both highly edible and easily shot when white man arrived in Australia, and even today people with no regard for our natural heritage shoot these birds. Bustards inhabit more arid environments, including grasslands, lightly timbered woodlands and open forests, where they feed upon grass seeds, fruits and many large insects, such as grasshoppers, as well as small reptiles and mammals.

Bush Thick-knee
Burhinus magnirostris

Most people of inland Australia are familiar with the haunting nocturnal wailing calls of this bird – known to many as 'curlew'. It lives in drier habitats and favours grassy areas with some woodland, and with leaf litter and debris for cover. Nesting birds sit out the daylight hours by keeping perfectly still, crouching and relying on cryptic plumage to conceal them. They will adopt a peculiar cryptic posture with head, neck, body and tail held flat against the ground to elim-inate any profile or shadows. If approached closer a defence posture is performed (**below**) and, as a last resort, the bird confronts the intruder with outstretched wings in a defensive bluff-attack run. They feed upon ground dwelling insects and other invertebrates.

The closely related Beach Thick-knee (see page 9) belongs to the same family as the Bush Thick-knee, the Burhinidae.

Bar-Shouldered Dove
Geopelia humeralis

This little pigeon (**left**) is usually encountered in pairs or small parties, but during the drier times of year may form groups of more than a hundred. It prefers woodlands with more shrub cover, and is thus more commonly found where woodland approaches other habitats such as pandanus swamp, melaleuca woodlands or mangroves; but does occur in more open forests. Food, consisting of seeds, is sought on the ground in open areas close to cover, to which the birds may flee. Other doves seen in similar habitats in this area include the Peaceful Dove and the Diamond Dove.

Squatter Pigeon
Petrophassa scripta

This sombrely coloured ground-dwelling pigeon (**below**) predominantly occurs in tropical Queensland, where it frequents grassy plains, sparser woodlands, dry watercourses and the modified country about homesteads and settlements. It will quickly become tame and confiding if regularly fed and not startled. Squatter Pigeons feed upon seeds taken from the ground, but will also take the odd insect. Another ground-dwelling pigeon, found on the south-east of the Peninsula only, is the larger Common Bronzewing, easily distinguishable from the Squatter by its larger size and far more extensive bronze markings on its wings.

Torresian Imperial Pigeon
Ducula spilorrhoa

Sadly, the above is now the official name of this lovely pigeon more commonly known as the Nutmeg or Torres Strait Pigeon. It migrates annually to the Australian tropics from New Guinea, arriving in about mid-August and departing during February and March. In Queensland this bird nests in large colonies in mangrove forests and rainforests on offshore islands. It also does nest in coastal mangroves on the mainland, sometimes in mainland rainforest and adajcent areas, and even in suburban gardens. The pair of parents raising their single young take turns each day to fly to-and-fro over the sea to the mainland tropical rainforests for tree and vine fruits. During the daytime, fruiting trees of Iron Range (**right**) and other vine forests on the Peninsula may abound with foraging pigeons.

To watch large flocks of these exquisite white birds purposefully and powerfully flying to their island nesting retreats (page iii) is a sight to behold and long-remember. It is one of the great ornithological experiences of life.

Wompoo Fruit-dove
Ptilinopus magnificus

This pigeon (**right below**) is one of the most splendid of all the lovely fruit doves.

On the Peninsula it inhabits vine forests and adjacent areas where suitable fruiting trees occur. The photograph was taken from a hide, some 14 metres above ground and from the fruiting tree, at Iron Range. Other fruit doves to visit this tree included the Superb Fruit-dove, the Rose-crowned Fruit-dove and the Torresian Imperial Pigeon (see above). The Palm Cockatoo photographed in its nest hole (**opposite**) was also taken from the very same hide.

Palm Cockatoo
Probosciger aterrimus

This magnificent parrot, the largest species of cockatoo, is widespread through New Guinea and, fortunately, occurs in the New Guinea-like lowland vine forests and adjacent eucalypt open-forests of the Peninsula, where it is not uncommon. As its huge and immensely powerful bill suggests, it feeds on the seeds of particularly tough fruits and nuts, such as those of pandanus trees. Birds nest in large tree hollows (**opposite**) or boughs or in broken off dead tree trunk stumps. Such large nesting hollows are not commonplace and nests may be used for many years, quite probably by the same birds.

Palm Cockatoos have been seen to perform most acrobatic displays including crest raising, flapping of extended open wings and leaning forward over a perch to hang inverted. Very recently birds have been observed displaying at a potential nesting site tree-hollow by banging the hollow bough with a piece of wood held in the foot, as a tool. Birds per-forming this remarkable behaviour may carry their 'drum stick' from one hollow to another; thus leaving no doubt that this is an example of the very rare phenomenon in animals other than humans of tool use!.

Red-tailed Black Cockatoo
Calyptorhynchus magnificus

The Red-tailed Black Cockatoo (**right**) is far more familiar to Australians than its larger relative the Palm Cockatoo, because it occurs widely throughout tropical Australia's north as well as over much of south-western, central and eastern Australia. Large flocks of this uniquely Australian cockatoo provide spectacular sights to visitors to the outback. Whilst by no means confined to Cape York Peninsula the Red-tailed Black Cockatoo is typical of it, being often seen by those travelling the long open roads of the Cape.

The other cockatoos typical of this region are the ubiquitous and much-loved Galah, living in the drier open country, and the Sulphur-crested, or White, Cockatoo which, in addition to the open country, also inhabits the vine forests. A tree we came to regularly sit and watch each sunset at Iron Range was the nightly roosting place of perhaps a thousand Sulphur-crested Cockatoos.

Golden-shouldered Parrot
Psephotus chrysopterygius

The Golden-shouldered Parrot (**opposite**) is fast becoming the Queensland symbol of an Australia-wide problem – the loss of uniquely Australian bird species to extinction. The conspicuous decline of this elegant parrot since the turn of the century has brought the species to sufficiently low numbers to cause grave concern. Undoubtedly, the capture of birds for the national and international live bird trade is to some degree responsible but is is highly likely that the recent modification of the birds habitat by fires and cattle grazing is a significant, if not major, contributing factor.

Golden-shouldered Parrots occur mostly in woodlands and open-forests in the centre and extreme south-west of the Peninsula, being most frequently encountered by bird-watchers in the Musgrave area. Birds nest by excavating a tunnel and terminal egg chamber into large termite mounds (see page 19) during April to June.

The Golden-shouldered Parrot is the closest living relative of the Paradise Parrot, a similar but even more brightly coloured parrot that used to be found inland south-east Queensland but is now thought to be extinct.

Red-winged Parrot
Aprosmictus erythropterus

The striking Red-winged Parrot (**right**) is a widespread species living throughout the Australian tropics, as well as the remainder of Queensland, central northern New South Wales, and southern New Guinea. Its loud penetrating sharp call notes and delightful undulating deeply flapping flight are characteristic of these areas of Australia. Although occurring extensively beyond Cape York Peninsula it is, like some of the cockatoos, part of the character of this region. This can also be said of such popular smaller parrots as the Rainbow and Scaly-breasted Lorikeets and the Pale-headed Rosella. The photograph shows a male bird in a native kapok tree.

Eclectus Parrot
Eclectus roratus

This is considered by many to be the most resplendent of Australia's parrot species, doubtless due in large part to its relative isolation on the Peninsula where it is restricted to Iron Range and McIlwraith Range areas. It lives in vine forests and adjacent eucalypt woodlands. So different are the two sexes that they were long thought to be of two different parrot species. Moreover, the sexual difference in this bird is extraordinary in that it is the red and blue female (upper left of front cover) that is the more colourful. The male is predominantly green with a little blue on the outer wings and bright red under them, and on the sides, which is only visible when the wings are raised in display (**right**) or in flight.

Eclectus Parrots are presently common where they occur, but continue to be threatened by the potential for significant habitat loss and by the illegal stealing of nestlings by dealers in the live bird trade. The species is, however, widespread throughout low-land New Guinea and numerous surrounding islands. Birds nest in natural tree hollows of larger forest and forest edge trees. As many as six pairs may nest in the same tree, often along with one or more pairs of Sulphur-crested Cockatoos.

Red-cheeked Parrot
Geoffroyus geoffroyi

This species has the same distributional range and occurs in the same habitats as the Eclectus Parrot. Males have a bright red face and forehead, a blue crown, and a red upper mandible. Females have a an olive-brown head and all grey bill.

Nesting takes place in a hollow tree spout, (**right**), or in a hole in a tree bough and the birds modify the entrance aperture by chewing about its perimeter, particularly above and below the hole. Pairs are often quite noisy about the nesting territory, the male bird often taking fast circular flights about the area and above the forest canopy whilst screaming loudly and continuously. The picture shows the female perched just prior to her feeding one of her two, almost-fledged, young. The male does not attend the nest, but feeds his mate closeby.

Double-eyed Fig-parrot
Psittaculirostris diophthalma

This (**page 20, above**) is Australia's smallest parrot. It has three distinct forms on the east coast of Australia, from Cape York Peninsula to northern New South Wales. The northern population is referred to as Marshall's Fig-parrot which the photograph, taken in the vine forests of Iron Range, depicts. These parrots are seed-eaters and feed mostly on figs. The picture shows a male, with much red about the face, and a female feeding on their basic diet of cluster fig seeds. They occur in vine forests, and adjacent melaleuca woodlands where their nest holes are often found. The birds excavate a hole in a rotten tree-trunk or a dead limb of a living tree.

Blue-winged Kookabuura
Dacelo leachii

Of all Australian birds kookaburras require the least introduction, being synonymous with the word Australia. The Blue-winged Kookaburra (**left**) and the, much better known, Laughing Kookaburra both occur on the Peninsula. They are in fact giant kingfishers but are unlike the typical kingfishers in feeding habits as well as size. Kookaburras feed upon a wide variety of prey including snakes, lizards, large insects, small mammals and the occasional small bird.

Both species can frequently be seen perched on the same roadside wires on the Peninsula. The Blue-winged Kookaburra is in fact the truly tropical representative, occurring throughout our tropics, and is a more colourful bird with extensive areas of blue on the wings, rump, and, in the male, tail. The tail of the female is red-brown with darker barring. Blue-winged kookaburras do not produce the amusing human-like laughter of their close relative, but give a more gutteral raucous squawking and screetching. They occur in woodlands, paperbark swamp and riverine vegetation. Whilst the Blue-winged Kookaburra occurs outside Australia, in southern New Guinea, our familiar Laughing Kookaburra is unique, or endemic, to continental Australia and Tasmania.

The photograph shows a male perched at the entrance to its nest hole, having just fed a Black Duck duckling to its nestlings.

Yellow-billed Kingfisher
Syma torotoro

Like so many of the birds peculiar within Australia to the wet forests of Cape York Peninsula, the Yellow-billed Kingfisher (**left**) is really a New Guinea species with a foot-hold Australian distribution. It is found in the heavy vine forest and adjacent woodland edges of the northern tip, Iron Range, Weipa and McIlwraith Range areas. This interesting forest kingfisher is not easily seen during the winter months, when it becomes relatively quiet and retiring. During the summer months of November to March it is, however, vocal and bold in the vicinity of its nest chambers which are dug into active termite mounds in trees. Of course this is the wet season, when few people are able to get to the haunts of this bird.

The kingfisher family is well represented on the Peninsula. In addition to the Yellow-billed, more typical of this region as a whole are found the Azure, Little, Forest, Red-backed, Sacred, Collared and, last but not least, the fabulous Buff-breasted Paradise Kingfisher (see page 50).

Buff-breasted Paradise-kingfisher
Tanysiptera sylvia

This splendid kingfisher was recently given its unwieldy name, to replace the better known White-tailed Kingfisher. Of the ten kinds of Australian kingfisher this is undoubtedly the most spectacular. It is one of eight paradise kingfishers, most of which occur in New Guinea and surrounding islands. Australia's tropical lowland rainforests are much enhanced every year by this beautifully feathered bird, which migrates south from New Guinea to breed in Australia. The birds arrive in early November and noisily establish small territories which must contain the bulbous termite mounds, usually on the ground, in which they will excavate a tunnel and nest chamber. The females, which have shorter central tail feathers, incubate the eggs and are then assisted by the male (**right**) in feeding one to three noisy young as they ceaselessly beg for insects, spiders, frogs and lizards. Young leave the nest in January or February quite capable of adequate flight. Once their offspring are independent of them the adult birds return to New Guinea, leaving the young birds to find their own way northward several weeks later.

Rainbow Bee-eater
Merops ornatus

Australia has only this single representative of the bee-eater family, which world-wide consists of twenty three colourful species. Many of the Australian birds, particularly in the south of their range, migrate to New Guinea for the winter whereas some northern birds are resident. In addition to woodlands, birds also frequent open country and may form huge night roosts in denser vegetation of heavy woodland, mangroves or rainforest. They nest by excavating a burrow into a bank or sandy soil and lay four to five eggs. Adults and young eat flying insects. The picture (**opposite above**) shows a long-tailed male, on the left, with a female.

Noisy Pitta
Pitta versicolor

Two pitta species commonly occur in the vine forests and thickets on the Peninsula, the Red-bellied Pitta and the larger Noisy Pitta (**opposite below**) which also occurs down the eastern Australian coastal zone to Sydney, New South Wales. The brightly coloured Noisy Pitta makes its presence in summer obvious by its loud and clearly whistled *walk-to-work* call, and will often be attracted to an observer mimicking the call. Some Noisy Pittas migrate to New Guinea each year, some move from highland breeding areas to lowland and offshore-island wintering grounds, and others simply remain resident all year round. The typical habitat is rainforest, but adjacent woodlands and mangroves are also used. Nesting takes place on the ground, in low vegetation or tree buttresses, the nest being a domed structure with a side entrance, often with a ramp of sticks, mosses and leaves as a 'doorstep'. The Red-bellied Pitta migrates from Cape York Peninsula to spend each winter in New Guinea, but some birds may remain here year-round.

Northern Scrub-robin
Drymodes superciliaris

This delicately cryptically marked and coloured bird (**right**) is another New Guinea species that has an apparently relict foot-hold distribution on Australia in the northern Cape York Peninsula vine forests and thickets. It used to also occur in the region of the Roper River of extreme eastern Northern Territory but now appears to be extinct there, possibly as a result of the repeated burning of its habitat.

The Northern Scrub-robin is very much a bird of the vine forest leaf-littered floor, although birds will perch several metres above the ground to sing. Their call is described as a long drawn-out whistle. The wonderfully cryptic plumage is most effective, the contrastingly adjacent black and white areas breaking the birds shape up to make it extremely difficult to locate when stationary.

The nest is most odd, consisting of a shallow cup of dead dry leaves and leaf pieces built upon the ground and lined with straw-like dry grasses and tendrils. This nest cup structure is surrounded by twigs, often surprisingly stout for the size of the bird, and many of these radiate out and down from the raised nest like the spokes of a wheel. A bird sitting tight on the nest is all but impossible to find, unless flushed by an extremely close approach.

Scrub-robins (there is a southern scrub-robin on the south of the Australian continent) were considered by some ornithologists to be members of the thrush family, but it is now generally conceded that they are most closely related to the Australian robins (which are not really robins at all, but are more correctly termed flycatchers; true robins, like the European Robin, are actually thrushes!).

White-faced Robin
Tregellasia leucops

Least known and encountered of the well known and much loved Australian robins is the White-faced; being confined to the tropical vine forests from the McIlwraith Range northwards. The strikingly contrasting white face and eye ring with black adjacent areas make this robin, the smallest species, a particularly appealing one. Visitors to these vine forests will find this an easy bird to see and watch, as it peers intensely at the forest floor for insect prey whilst clinging to the vertical stem of a sapling or to the side of a tree trunk. The delightfully compact and neat cup nest of this diminutive robin (**right**) is sometimes in a sapling fork only a couple of metres above the ground, but as the birds are sensitive when nesting they should not be approached too closely.

A close relative that may be seen together in the White-faced Robin habitat, or immediately adjacent to it, is the White-browed Robin. It is a much larger bird that occurs throughout much of the Australian tropical zone, but which is more closely associated with lower vegetation and the forest floor, and also lives in eucalypt woodland. Another flycatcher confined mostly to these vine forests is the Yellow-legged Flycatcher. It is a much rarer flycatcher than the White-faced, occurring from the Claudie River at Iron Range northwards. Both species are found in New Guinea. The Lemon-breasted Flycatcher is another quite closely related flycatcher that can be seen in the same area as the White-faced Robin, but is also found southward to the central coastal Queensland coast, and in Arnhemland.

Yellow-breasted Boatbill
Machaerirhynchus flaviventer

The Yellow-breasted Boatbill is the most peculiar of our Australian flycatchers, its very broadly flattened beak being a quite unique adaptation that is apparently for snatching flying insects. Its tiny suspended nest is extremely difficult to find and as it may be built between four to twenty metres above ground, a lot of luck is required to find one low enough to study and photograph. Seen here is the male bird (**left**), the female is a much lighter and duller yellow and is olive on the back where he is black. Some nesting females retain the distinctly barred immature ventral plumage, as was the case in the Iron Range nest photographed. Normally dressed females have pure yellow underparts.

In addition to the boatbill, the robins and the monarchs, there are the fan-tailed flycatchers, or fantails as they are known. The best known of the Australian fantails is the Willie Wagtail, which occurs throughout Australia, although much sparser on northern Cape York Peninsula. All of the other three fantails found in Australia, the Grey, Rufous and Northern, occur on the Peninsula, but the Northern is the truly tropical one. It is rather similar to the ubiquitous Grey Fantail but is larger, perches more vertically upright and is spotted white on its grey chest.

Frilled Monarch
Arses telescophthalmus

The Frilled Monarch is a bird of the New Guinea lowlands and also occurs in vine forests of northern Cape York Peninsula, south to the McIlwraith Range. This rarely photographed bird (**left**) is one of eleven Australian birds known collectively as monarch flycatchers, of which all except the Pied Monarch Flycatcher occur on the Peninsula. The Black-winged Monarch is another monarch confined to this region but it is found only from the Claudie River at Iron Range northwards.

The Frilled Monarch is very similar to its southern close relative the Pied Monarch of the Atherton Region which can be found in forest of the Cooktown to Townsville area. Like the Pied Monarch the sexes of the Frilled Monarch differ, the chin of the male being black whereas it is white in the female. Bare orbital pale blue skin in both sexes, of both species, gives these birds a particularly attractive look.

The nests of the Frilled and Pied Monarchs are distinctly different to those of other Australian monarch flycatchers, being delicate and beautiful frail cup-shaped baskets of fine dry twiglets, rootlets and vine tendrils loosely woven and bound together with spider webs and decorated on the outside with pieces of lichen. These structures are slung, hammock-like, between vertical hanging vine stems. Two eggs form the clutch and are laid mostly between September and January. Both the Frilled and Pied monarchs are active birds, ceaselessly foraging for insect prey on tree trunks and larger boughs, clinging to the bark and clambering and fluttering upwards and downwards.

Little Shrike-thrush
Colluricincla megarhyncha

The Little, or Rufous as it is sometimes called, Shrike-thrush (**right**) is one of four shrike-thrushes found in Australia. Only this species and the Australia-wide Grey Shrike-thrush occur on Cape York Peninsula, and both also occur in New Guinea. Little Shrike-thrushes are found throughout Cape York Peninsula, on the Gulf of Carpentaria, throughout Arnhemland, and down eastern coastal Australia into north-eastern New South Wales. The Arnhemland birds used to be recognised as a separate species, but there is now no doubt they are mere forms of one species. On the Peninsula they are commonly seen in the vine forests, paperbark swamps, in vegetation along rivers and creeks, coastal open-forests and in mangroves. The larger Grey Shrike-thrush favours more open drier wooded areas.

Other than this birds musical song, it is often the sound of foraging birds tearing into dead dry foliage that attracts the observers attention. In such places the bird seeks out insects and spiders. It may also take on larger prey, such as frogs and nestling birds.

Shrike-thrushes are very closely related to the Australian whistlers, and are in fact little more than large whistlers. The closely related, predominantly tropical, Mangrove Golden Whistler and Grey Whistler also occur in this region; as well as the Rufous Whistler which is widespread throughout Australia.

Lovely Fairy-wren
Malurus amabilis

This charming little bird (**right**) lives amongst dense low undergrowth on the margins of vine forests, woodlands, open-forests, dune-vegetation, along watercourses and rank roadside grasses and weeds. On the west coast of the Peninsula it occurs as far south as Edward River but on the east its range extends down the coast almost to Townsville.

The only other fairy-wren living on Cape York Peninsula is the the Red-backed Fairy-wren. The magnificent adult male of this species is a glossy jet black bird with brownish wings and a deep iridescent blood red back. The female, and young males, is a drab pale brown bird with a white throat. This fine bird species is not found together with the Lovely Fairy-wren, as it occupies the grassy understorey of woodlands. Its range includes the entire tropical north and the east of Queensland and northern New South Wales.

Fairy Gerygone
Gerygone palpebrosa

The Fairy Gerygone (pronounced gerry-gon-ee) is a warbler very widely distributed through New Guinea that is found in Australia. The males of birds from the Peninsula (**left**) differ from those further south in having a dark chin that extends down the central throat and then around either side of the neck to join the dark ear coverts, thus forming a white 'moustache'. Southern males merely have a chin smudged blackish, on an otherwise white throat.

Fairy Gerygones are found living in rainforest, rainforest margins, wetter vegetation along rivers and the landward edge of mangroves. During the nesting season a pair alone attend the domed nest, suspended from a twig, with a small porch or hood over the entrance hole. The most intriguing aspect of this birds nesting activity is that it almost invariably, in this region anyway, builds its nest immediately adjacent to an actively used nest of stinging wasps. The wasps obviously do not disturb or harm the birds and, whilst it seems that the birds gain some protection from the wasps, it is not at all clear what the wasps gain from this arrangement.

Another tropical gerygone widespread over the Peninsula is the similar-sized Large-billed Warbler, which inhabits similar, wetter habitats to the Fairy Gerygone. This is a less colourful bird, however, being generally brownish above, whitish below and with a buff wash on the sides of the breast. A fine semicircle of white feathers arches over and beneath the eye. This warbler's range extends down the east Queensland coast to near Rockhampton, and it also lives in Arnhemland and the Kimberley.

Yellow-bellied Sunbird
Nectarinia jugularis

The predominantly tropical Sunbird (**left**) is the only Australian representative of the extremely colourful approximately 118 species of sunbirds that occur from Africa through Asia to Australasia. Whilst the females are generally dressed in yellows and olives or browns the males are quite resplendent. The male Yellow-bellied sports a breast and throat of iridescent metallic blue-black.

Our sunbird is found in many habitats including woodlands, mangroves, coastal scrub, vine forest margins, and is a familiar sight in gardens. The Yellow-bellied Sunbird's Australian distribution is the same as that of the Fairy Gerygone (see above) except that it does occur further down the west coast of the Peninsula, almost to the Gulf of Carpentaria.

The Sunbird is a familiar and much-loved species wherever it occurs close to human habitation. In addition to frequenting flowering and fruiting plants immediately about homes and gardens for nectar and fruit pulp or juices, it will often build its lovely tear-shaped pendulous nest beneath the eaves of a verandah or house walls, attached to a hanging piece of string or wire. The bright yellow female (**left**) nest builds, dashing back and forth with pieces of fine material, with her colourful mate closely following or singing from a vantage point nearby. The female alone incubates the clutch of two or three eggs, but the male assists in feeding the nestlings.

Tawny-breasted Honeyeater
Xanthotis flaviventer

Of Australia's approximately sixty six honeyeater species, the Tawny-breasted is one of the least studied because of its relative inaccessibility. It occurs only in the vine forests and thickets and adjacent woodlands on northern Cape York Peninsula, southward to the Archer River area on the west and to the McIlwraith Range on the east. It is a difficult bird to see in the forest as it lives mostly in canopy and sub-canopy strata, where it gleans insects from foliage, trunks and dead leaves as well as feeding upon flower nectar and some fruits.

It is doubtful that photographs of free-living wild Australian birds have been previously published, and the accompanying photograph (**right**) is certainly the first published of the species at the nest. Very few nests indeed have ever been found. The nest is typical of the honeyeater family, in being a suspended 'hammock' cup nest consisting of fine and light materials. The particular nest photographed was built into the upper canopy foliage of a small, ten metre tall, roadside tree that was thickly covered in leafy vine tendrils.

Like so many of the birds peculiar to Cape York Peninsula, within Australia, this is one of those species which is really a bird of the New Guinea avifauna that has a foot-hold Australian distribution on the northern Cape. Its only really close relative within Australia is Macleay's Honeyeater of the Atherton Region, which is approximately from Cooktown to Paluma near Townsville.

Graceful Honeyeater
Meliphaga gracilis

This is yet another exclusively tropical honeyeater that occurs together with a very closely related species, the Yellow-spotted Honeyeater, on Cape York Peninsula. The Graceful and the Yellow-spotted Honeyeaters are similar in their appearance but the former is slightly smaller, paler below and has a proportionately longer and slimmer bill than the latter. Both species have an identical distribution in Australia from northern Cape York southward to Townsville, Queensland; but whilst the Graceful Honeyeater is found also in New Guinea, the Yellow-spotted is uniquely Australian.

The Graceful Honeyeater (**right**) dwells mostly within vine forests and thickets and adjacent eucalypt woodlands, where it feeds on small berries, flower nectar, insects and spiders and is often seen around flowering trees in the company of other honeyeaters. Other honeyeaters to be seen commonly on Cape York Peninsula in places are: Helmeted, Silver-crowned, Noisy and Little Friarbirds, Blue-faced, Varied, White-gaped, Yellow (see page 57), Black-chinned, White-throated, Green-backed, Brown, White-streaked, Brown-backed, Bar-breasted, Rufous-banded, Rufous-throated, Banded, Dusky, Red-headed and of course the Tawny-breasted (see above) honeyeaters.

Yellow Honeyeater
Lichenostomus flavus

The Yellow Honeyeater (**left**) is an exclusively tropical species of endemic Australian bird, being widespread in a variety of habitats throughout Cape York Peninsula southward almost to Rockhampton on the Queensland coast. It occurs predominantly in woodlands and open-forests. Australian honeyeaters, of the family Meliphagidae, have evolved and diversified in large part to take advantage of the nectar available from Australia's, often peculiar, flowering flora, and the rich smaller insect life. They can, to some extent, be considered as Australia's ecological equivalent to the numerous sunbirds of Africa and Asia and the hummingbirds of South America.

Flowering eucalypts, melaleucas, acacias, banksias, grevilleas and leptospermums provide a rich source of nectar for these birds to feed upon, in addition the flowers often attracting suitable insects to the area of the flowers for the birds to eat. Honeyeaters feed mostly upon insects and nectar from these blossoms, as well as on small berries.

Until very recently the Yellow Honeyeater remained a very little known species, due to its predominantly tropical range. Recently, however, some study of the dense populations in Townsville city suburbs has brought to light some of its private life. Social and nesting groups may consist of more than just a pair and younger birds may assist the adult pair in their nesting attempts as 'helpers'.

Red-browed Firetail
Emblema temporalis

Finches are popular cage birds and the Red-browed Firetail is certainly no exception, being widely available as an aviculturally bred species. Red-browed Firetails live in rainforest clearings, eucalypt forests and woodlands, heathlands, mangroves and in suburban areas. When not breeding birds may form flocks of several hundred birds, but when nesting pairs may remain alone or several pairs may nest in loose association. The bird feeds mostly upon grass seeds but also takes some other plant seeds, some small fruits, and some insects. Fluctuations in bird numbers clearly relate to seeding grass availability. An un-mown larger suburban garden lawn may be sufficient to encourage a pair to nest-build and reproduce.

Whilst this beautiful finch (**left**) extends down the east of Queensland and New South Wales and throughout most of Victoria to the Adelaide region of South Australia, and is introduced to the south-west of the continent, it is found throughout Cape York Peninsula. Of the eighteen Australian finches, only three are found throughout much of this region, these being the Double-barred and Black-throated Finches and the Chestnut-breasted Mannikin. In addition, the Star, Crimson and Masked Finches and the Pictorella Mannikin may be seen in some southern areas of the Peninsula only. Sadly, the infamous pest finch, the House Sparrow, is now also widely established in parts of this tropical wilderness.

Black Butcherbird
Cracticus quoyi

Six of the eight Australian butcherbirds, which includes our familiar magpies, currawongs and butcherbirds, occur on Cape York Peninsula. Only this species (**right**) and the Black-backed Butcherbird are exclusively tropical, but both also live in New Guinea. The Black Butcherbird has a large powerful beak, viciously tipped with a hook, for capturing its animal foods of birds, reptiles, frogs, insects, and some fruit. Like its relatives, it often takes larger prey to a thorn or to a tree crevice to spike or wedge it in order to be able to tear it into manageable pieces for itself or its young. It dwells within vine forests, woodlands and mangroves.

Metallic Starling
Aplonis metallica

Also called the Shining Starling, this (**opposite above**) is the only member of the large old world starling family native to Australia. It migrates from New Guinea to tropical north-eastern Queensland each year (July to September) to breed; returning north between February and April. It builds hanging pear-shaped nests of twigs and tendrils suspended from a tree branch with a side entrance partly obscured by a funnel or spout, unlike the majority of starlings which nest in holes. It is gregarious when breeding, nesting in colonies of up to hundreds of nests.

Yellow Oriole
Oriolus flavocinctus

All three members of the oriole family in Australia occur on the Peninsula. The Yellow Oriole (**right**) is exclusively tropical but the Olive-backed Oriole and Figbird occur throughout most or much of eastern Australia respectively. The Yellow Oriole is a bird of mangroves, swamp woodland and vine forest creeks. It is an Australian species with a foot-hold distribution in southern New Guinea, contrary to the situation in numerous other birds. Its distinctive powerful loud bubbling call of 3 to 4 varied notes are characteristic where pairs are in residence. It feeds almost exclusively on tropical fruits, but doubtless feeds young birds some insect foods.

Magnifcent Riflebird
Ptiloris magnificus

Three of the four birds of paradise found in Australia are riflebirds, the fourth being the Trumpet Manucode (see page 61). The Magnificent Riflebird (**opposie below**) is the most northern and largest, of the rainforest-dwelling riflebirds; which constitute three isolated species populations down the eastern coastal area of Queensland.

Riflebirds are typical birds of paradise. The ornate males are promiscuous birds that call from and display on a few courtship perches within their territory. Females visit males, compare them, and select the finest to mate with. Females alone build the nest and care for the eggs and young.

Trumpet Manucode
Manucodia keraudrenii

The Trumpet Manucode (**opposite above**), a New Guinea bird also found on Cape York Peninsula, is a true bird of paradise. Unlike most birds of paradise, however, this bird forms monogamous pairs to nest, in vine forests and rainforests. We believe this is the first published colour photograph of a wild bird taken in Australia, if not anywhere. This bird often builds its nest near to that of the aggressive Black Butcherbird (see page 58), apparently for protection.

Great Bowerbird
Chlamydera nuchalis

There are nineteen species of bowerbirds of which ten are found in Australia and eleven in New Guinea, two species occurring in both. Of bowerbirds on Cape York the Fawn-breasted Bowerbird (**left**) is found only on north-eastern Cape York Peninsula in Australia, but also lives in New Guinea; the Spotted Catbird is restricted to tropical eastern Queensland with one population on eastern Cape York Peninsula and another in the Atherton Region, but also lives in New Guinea; and the Great Bowerbird (**opposite below**) only occurs throughout the Australian tropics.

The Great Bowerbird, largest member of the family, is a bird of eucalypt woodland, riverine vegetation and drier scrubs. Males build an 'avenue' bower of two parallel walls of sticks. The bower is constructed solely to impress potential mates, and perhaps also to deter rival males. Males are promiscuous and spend the breeding season calling and displaying at their bowers in an attempt to mate with many females. Females will then nest build, incubate their one or two eggs, and raise young entirely alone.

Fawn-breasted Bowerbird
Chlamydera cerviniventris

The Fawn-breasted Bowerbird (**left**) frequents eucalypt-melaleuca woodland, vine scrubs, riverine thickets, grasslands and mangrove fringes. Male Fawn-breasted Bowerbirds build 'avenue' bowers, but build their parallel vertical walls atop a very substantial raised platform-like pile of sticks.

Unlike adult male Great Bowerbirds, male Fawn-breasted Bowerbirds do not have a lilac crest, the bird being entirely dusky-brown above. It is of the greatest interest, therefore, that when courting a female in the bower avenue the male presents his nape to her, by turning his beak away, often with something held in it. As can be seen in the pictures of the Fawn-breasted (**left**) and the Great Bowerbird (**opposite below**) this courtship posture is identical, but whilst in the later it presents the female with a brightly coloured nape it shows nothing to advantage in the Fawn-breasted. This is convincing evidence that the Fawn-breasted is a bird in which males did once have a coloured nape crest which they have lost, probably because their more complex bower has replaced it as a display object, but they have not yet lost the posture that presents it to the female!

MAMMALS

Some sixty nine species of mammals, excluding recently introduced species and marine mammals, have been recorded on Cape York Peninsula: one monotreme (the Short-beaked Echidna), twenty seven marsupials, and forty two placental mammals of which twenty eight are bat species. About thirty eight of these species are exclusively tropical, or very predominantly so, and occur on the Peninsula and to areas south of it, and some also live in New Guinea. Mammals, such as the Dingo (see page 68), are widespread throughout Australia whereas others are confined to the Peninsula. The Spotted Cuscus and the Grey Cuscus (see page 64) are restricted to Cape York Peninsula, but are more widespread in New Guinea. The Cinnamon Antechinus, and the Cape York Melomys (see page 68) are endemic and do not occur elsewhere.

 ## Northern Quoll
Dasyurus hallucatus

This quoll (**opposite above**) occurs mostly in drier rocky areas with sparse vegetation where it predates small mammals such as antechinuses, reptiles and insects; as well as eating figs and other soft fruits. Quolls belong to the group of carnivorous marsupials called the dasyurids, which also includes the much smaller dunnarts, phascogales, antechinuses and planigales. All are represented by one, or two, species on the Peninsula, the most common being the Red-cheeked Dunnart.

 ## Northern Brown Bandicoot
Isoodon macrourus

Bandicoots belong to a group of marsupials called perameloids, which also includes the bilbies of arid central Australia. The Northern Brown Bandicoot (**opposite below**) is the most widespread of the four bandicoot species found on the Peninsula. It inhabits woodlands, open-forests and grasslands. At night it forages for earthworms, spiders, insects, or berries; but during the day it hides-up in hollow logs, grassy tussocks or in a shallow depression which it covers with a heap of ground litter.

 ## Striped Possum
Dactylopsila trivirgata

This mammal (**left**) is confined to tropical rainforests and adjacent woodlands from northern Cape York south to Paluma as well occurring in New Guinea. During the day it rests in a leafy nest inside a tree hollow or amongst a clump of epiphytes. At night it forages for wood-boring grubs and other insects on tree trunks and amongst fallen rotting logs. It uses its two long bayonet-like lower incisors to gouge away bark and expose prey which it then extracts with its its long tongue, or probes out using the sharp claw on its elongated fourth finger. It also feeds on leaves and fruits.
The Striped Possum belongs to the group of possums called petaurids, which includes the Common Ringtail Possum and Sugar Glider (see page 64); both of which are common on the Peninsula.

Sugar Glider
Petaurus breviceps

As its name suggests, the Sugar Glider (**opposite above**) is extremely agile and can glide, or volplane, for at least fifty metres. To take-off it thrusts with its hindlegs and leaps forwards into the air, immediately spreading out flaps of skin, or membranes, at either side of its body to assist 'flight'. To land it folds its hindlegs in towards its body and with a final upward swoop lands on all fours! Sugar Gliders favour eucalypt woodlands where tree hollows are available for shelter and there is an abundant food source of eucalyptus sap and acacia gum.

Spotted Cuscus
Phalanger maculatus

The Spotted Cuscus (**right**) occurs mostly in vine forests and their margins, although it has been seen in nypa palms of mangroves (see page 10) and in paperbarks near river banks. During the day cuscuses are sluggish and sloth-like and spend most of their time sleeping amongst the leafy canopy with their tails coiled beneath them. At night, however, they are surprisingly active, moving about the leafy canopy to forage on leaves and fruits. The Spotted Cuscus supplements its diet with animal protein and will eat insects and birds eggs and nestlings. When climbing the prehensile tail is uncoiled to aid balance and the bare scaly tail tip is well adapted for curling around and gripping branches for additional support. Male Spotted Cuscus are easy to recognise as, unlike the plain grey females, their grey fur is blotched and spotted white – hence the common name. Skin colour is a pinkish-yellow and the ears are small, barely protruding above the fur. Indeed, it was the small rounded ears and the large, forward-facing, staring eyes of this species that led early settlers to believe it was a monkey!

Grey Cuscus
Phalanger orientalis

Grey Cuscus (**opposite below**) of both sexes are uniformly greyish-brown and have a darker area of fur running down the central back. Unlike the Spotted, the skin of the Grey Cuscus is greyish, and it is of a lighter build and has a longer snout and larger, more prominent, ears. The Grey Cuscus has only been recorded from the vine forests of McIlwraith Range and Iron Range. It is predominantly herbivorous unlike the Spotted which has a more mixed, or omnivorous, diet.

Female cuscuses have a permanent, forwardly opening, pouch which encloses four nipples. Like all marsupials, newly born young are embryonic-looking, being minute, blind, and hairless with poorly developed hindlimbs. After birth they crawl into their mother's pouch and cling with the sharp, curved, claws on their forelegs to her nipples to suckle milk. One to three pouch young have been recorded, but only one of them is reared.

Cuscuses belong to the group of possums called the phalangerids, which also include brushtails. The Common Brushtail Possum is sparsely distributed in the central and southern areas of Cape York Peninsula where it inhabits open-forests and woodlands.

Agile Wallaby
Macropus agilis

The Agile Wallaby (**opposite above**) is commonly seen on the Peninsula. It inhabits woodlands, open-forests, and grasslands mostly close to creeks and lagoons where there is plenty of grass for it to feed upon. Small groups of them often aggregate in suitable feeding areas. The Agile is easily recognised from other wallabies by the lighter stripe of fur along its thighs, the black tip to its ears and tail, and the median dark brown stripe between the eyes. The Northern Nailtail Wallaby and the Swamp Wallaby also occur on the Peninsula but are mostly solitary and are active only between dawn and dusk.

Antilopine Wallaroo
Macropus antilopinus

The Antilopine Wallaroo (**opposite below**) occurs mainly in eucalypt woodlands with a grassy understory. On very hot days groups of them seek refuge in the shade of trees or under bushes, usually close to a waterhole, and only venture out to forage when it is cooler. It is often mistakenly called a Red Kangaroo, on account of its large size and reddish-brown fur. The Red Kangaroo is not found on the Peninsula. The Antilopine lacks distinctive facial markings. The Common Wallaroo and the Eastern Grey Kangaroo occur in the south-east corner of the Peninsula.

Spectacled Flying-fox
Pteropus conspicillatus

The Spectacled Flying-fox (**left above**) has a prominent pale straw-coloured fur around its eyes that suggests a pair of spectacles – hence its name. At night flying-foxes embark on forays to feed on nectar and pollen from blossoms and fruits of forest trees and palms. Daytime is spent in communal 'camps'. Camps are found in the upper canopy of a tall tree, or trees, in vine forest, woodland swamps or mangroves. It is easy to locate camps as these bats spend much time squawking amongst themselves. Some camps, such as those of the Little Red Flying-fox, also found on the Peninsula, may consist of more than 100,000 individuals!

Large-eared Horseshoe-bat
Rhinolophus philippinensis

A great diversity of insectivorous bats occur on the Peninsula, including ghost, sheathtail, mastiff, bent-wing and horseshoe bats. Like all horseshoe bats, this species (**left**) has an elaborate noseleaf, the U-shaped lower part resembling a horseshoe. Its precise function is not fully understood but it may direct the high frequency signals these bats emit. They detect prey such as moths and other flying insects, by using ultrasonic 'sonar' calls which bounce off objects and return signals to their sensitive ears. In the daytime it roosts in relatively small colonies in caves and mine shafts.

Cape York Melomys
Melomys capensis

The Cape York Melomys (**right**) is restricted to the Peninsula, mostly on the east coast. It inhabits vine forests and adjacent margins. It is predominantly a tree climber. Its long shiny hairless tail and broad hind feet are well adapted for its arboreal existence and its typically rodent pair of incisor teeth efficiently gnaw through fruit, seed and occasional insect foods.

The Cape York Rat may also be encountered at night foraging amongst leaf litter for nuts, fruits and insects in vine forests. Unlike the melomyses, with which it is often associated, it does not climb trees. The larger White-tailed Rat is, however, a competent tree climber which, in addition to plant foods, also eats insects, amphibians, small reptiles and bird eggs. Other native rodents include water-rats, melomyses, tree-rats (see below), rock-rats, prehensile- tailed rats, mice and hopping-mice. Representative species of each of these groups are found on the Peninsula.

Black-footed Tree-rat
Mesembriomys gouldii

The handsome Black-footed Tree-rat (**right below**) is one of Australia's largest rodents. It inhabits woodlands and open-forests, particularly eucalypt forests, with a grassy understorey. During the day it rests in tree hollows but at night it prowls around in search of flowers, seeds and fruits. It appears to be particularly fond of fruits of pandanus trees.

Dingo
Canis familiaris

The Dingo is perhaps one of the most familiar of all Australian mammals, being widespread throughout much of the continent. It is related to the primitive dogs of New Guinea, south-eastern Asia and northern Africa and, although its origins are unknown, it is thought to have been introduced by Aboriginal people. Fossil records show it has been here for at least 8000 years. The Dingo and the domestic dog are the same species and can interbreed; the Dingo breeds once a year whilst domestic dogs can reproduce twice. Most dingoes are a pale sandy colour (**back cover**) but some may be reddish and others, particularly those dwelling within rainforests, may even be black and tan.

Dingoes inhabit grasslands, woodlands, heathlands and also forest edges where they hunt wallabies, rodents, birds, and reptiles. Dingoes have long been regarded as a pest by graziers because sick or young sheep and cattle are included in their diet. Dingoes are considered to be an introduced pest species, particularly by graziers, and to be detrimental to both stock animals and native wildlife. Studies have shown, however, livestock may comprise as little as two percent of some dingoes' diet. The far more recently 'introduced' white human is undoubtedly far more detrimental to Australia's landscape and wildlife than are dingoes. Unlike the dogs, however, we have the ability to try and redress past mistakes and prevent future ones.

Further Reading

BROCK, J. 1986	Top End Native Plants John Brock, Darwin
COGGER, H.G. 1986	Reptiles and Amphibians of Australia Fourth edition, Reed, Sydney
COMMON, I.F.B. & WATERHOUSE, D.F. 1981	Butterflies of Australia 2nd edition, Angus & Robertson, Melbourne
LAVARACK, P.S. & GRAY, B. 1985	Tropical Orchids of Australia Nelson, Melbourne
PIZZEY, G. 1980	A Field Guide to the Birds of Australia Collins, Sydney
READERS DIGEST SERVICES 1988	Readers Digest Complete Book of Australian Birds 2nd edition, Readers Digest, Sydney
SLATER, P.,SLATER, P. & SLATER, R. 1986	The Slater Field Guide to Australian Birds Weldon, Sydney
STRAHAN, R 1983	The Australian Museum Complete Book of Australian Mammals Angus & Robertson, Sydney

Photographic Credits

(abbreviations following page numbers are : a = above, b = below)

KERRY TRAPNELL:	Three front cover scenics, ii, 3, 4a & b, 5a & b, 6a & b, 7a & b, 8a & b, 9b, 11b, 12a & b, 13b, 16b, 18, 19, 20b
STANLEY BREEDEN	47, 62a, 63, 68b
IAN MORRIS	46a & b
RALPH & DAPHNE KELLER/ A.N.T. Photo Library	41a
BELINDA WRIGHT	66b.
CLIFF & DAWN FRITH	All other photographs.

Acknowledgements

We thank John Young for his invaluable skills at Iron Range in finding and accessing nests of rarely photographed and endemic Cape York Peninsula birds. We thank staff of Queensland National Parks and Wildlife Service for support, particularly Mike Delaney and Mark Geyle. Sincere thanks to Peter Stanton for kindly writing the Foreword and commenting on our Introduction and Habitat text. Grateful thanks to Peter Valentine for permission to reproduce his, modified, butterfly text.

For hospitality, valued company, the provision of photographic subjects and help in other ways we thank Robbie and Judy Bredl; Robyn and Rolly Clarke; Bill and Wendy Cooper; Sam and Lisa Dibella; Bill Laverack; the McCullough family; Keith MacDonald; Anita and Ross Pope; Rupert Russell;

Andrew Taplin; Jeff and Jo McClure; Dave Thompson; Margaret and, the late, Arthur Thorsborne; Nick Took; Peter and Valerie Valentine; and John Winter.

We particularly thank Kerry Trapnell; Stanley Breeden; Ian Morris; Ralph and Daffi Keller; and Belinda Wright for contributing their photographs.

Our own photographs were taken with OLYMPUS OM-4 cameras, accessories and Zuiko lenses with OLYMPUS and METZ flash systems. Camera and flash systems supplied by GUNZ (Photographic) Pty. Ltd. of Sydney, with particular thanks to Bob Pattie.
Most film used was Kodachrome 64 KR 135.

Typesetting & Finished Artwork by Law Design Pty Ltd   Printed by Inprint Limited, Australia

Index to Plants and Animals

(Page numbers in boldface are those subjects illustrated)

Acacia	15, 16
Antechinus, Cinnamon	20, 63
Ant-plant	**16**
Ant	10, 12, 16, 25
Bandicoot	15, 62 - 63
Northern Brown	**62**, 63
Banksia	13, 16
Bee-eater, Rainbow	50, **51**
Boatbill, Yellow-breasted	**53**
Bowerbird, Fawn-breasted	**61**
Great	**60**, 61
Brolga	**38**
Brush-turkey, Australian	40, **41**
Bustard, Australian	**42**
Butcherbird, Black	**58**, 61
Black-backed	58
Butterfly	15, 16, 22 - 25
Birdwing	**23**
Common Australian Crow	**24**, 25
Fiery Jewel	**25**
Fivebar Swordtail	**22**
Hamadryad	**25**
Northern Jezabel	**24**, 25
Orange Dart	**22**
Red-bodied Swallowtail	**23**
Cassowary, Southern	20, **36**
Casuarina	9, 16
Catbird, Spotted	61
Cockatoo	44 - 46
Palm	16, 20, 36, 44, **45**
Red-tailed Black	**44**
Sulphur-crested	46, 48
Convolvulus, Goat's Foot	**8**, 9
Crane, Sarus	38, **39**
Crocodile	10, 27 - 29, 67
Estaurine	10, **29**
Freshwater	**28**, 29
Cuckoo, Chestnut-breasted	**36**
Cuscus, Grey	20, 63, 64, **65**
Spotted	20, 63, **64**
Dingo	15, 63, 68, **back cover**
Dotterel, Red-capped	9
Dove	43
Bar-shouldered	**43**
Duck	38
Plumed Whistling	**38**
Echidna	63
Eucalyptus	2, 13, 15, **18**, 19
Fairy-wren, Lovely	**54**
Red-backed	54
Fantail	53
Fenslia	**9**, 13
Fig, Cluster	**20**, 67
Figbird	58
Fig-parrot, Double-eyed	**20**
Finch	57
Firetail, Red-browed	**57**
Flycatcher	36, 52 - 53
Flying-fox	15, 67
Spectacled	**67**

Frog	26
Giant Tree	**26**
Wood	**26**
Frogmouth	40
Fruit-dove	44
Wompoo	**44**
Gecko	27
Ring-tailed	**27**
Gerygone, Fairy	**55**
Glider, Sugar	64, **65**
Goose, Magpie	37, **38**
Grass, Hairy Spinifex	9
Grevillea	13, 15, 16
Heron, Great-billed	10, **37**
Pied	37
Honeyeater	15, 36, 56 - 57
Graceful	**56**
Tawny-breasted	**56**
Yellow	56, **57**
White-streaked	36
Horseshoe-bat, Large-eared	**67**
Kangaroo	15, 67
Kapok	16, 46
Kingfisher	49
Buff-breasted Paradise	19, 20, 49, **50**
Yellow-billed	19, 20, 36, **49**
Kite, Black	**40**
Whistling	40
Kookaburra, Blue-winged	**49**
Laughing	49
Leptospermum	13
Lily, Cape York	**16**
Lizard	15, 27, 30 - 31
Frilled	**30**
Lorikeet	15, 46
Mangrove	10, **11**, 12
Manucode, Trumpet	36, 58, **60**, 61
Melaleuca	**14**, 13 - 16
Melomys, Cape York	63, **68**
Monarch	36, 53
Frilled	36, **53**
Monitor	15, 27, 30 - 31
Gould's Goanna	**30**
Mangrove	10, **31**
Merten's	**31**
Nightjar	40
Orchid	15, 20
Black	**15**
Tea Tree	**15**
Oriole	58
Yellow	**58**
Owl, Rufous	**40**
Owlet-nightjar	**40**
Pandanus	7, 9, 10, 16, **17**, 20
Palm, Corypha	**10**
Mangrove	**10**
Parrot	44 - 48
Eclectus	**front cover**, 20, 36, **48**
Golden-shouldered	19, 26, 46, **47**
Red-cheeked	36, **48**

Parrot (Continued)	
Red-winged	**46**
Pigeon	43 - 44
Squatter	**43**
Torresian Imperial	**iii**, 20, **44**
Pitta, Noisy	50, **51**
Red-bellied	36, 50
Plant, Cape York Heath	13
Insectivorous	12, 13
Pitcher	**12**, 13
Possum	15, 63 - 65
Striped	20, **63**
Python	32 - 33
Amethystine	**32**, 33
Green	20, **32**, 33
Olive	33
Water	33
Quoll, Northern	**62**, 63
Riflebird	58, 59
Magnificent	36, 58, **59**
Robin, White-faced	36, **52**
Scrubfowl, Orange-footed	**41**
Scrub-robin, Northern	36, **52**
Scrubwren, Tropical	36
Shrike-thrush, Grey	54
Little	**54**
Skink	27
Jewel	**27**
Snake	15, 27, 32 - 35
Brown Tree	**34**
Northern Tree	**34**
Papuan Black Whip	**35**
Taipan	**35**
Stork, Black-necked	**36**, 37
Starling, Metallic	58, **59**
Sunbird, Yellow-bellied	**55**
Termite	**front cover, ii, 5, 19**, 46, 49, 50
Thick-knee, Beach	9, 42
Bush	**42**
Tortoise	27 - 29
New-Guinea Snake-necked	**28**, 29
Tree, Grass	16, **19**
Tree-rat, Black-footed	16, **68**
Wallaby	15, 66 - 67
Agile	**66**, 67
Wallaroo	15, 66 - 67
Antilopine	**66**, 67
Warbler, Large-billed	55
Waterbird	10, 37 - 38
Whistler	54

70